D1069259

The Benjamin PSI Series

Consulting Editors

Fred S. Keller

Ben A. Green, Jr.

W. A. Benjamin, Inc.

**Menlo Park, California • Reading, Massachusetts • London •
Amsterdam • Don Mills, Ontario • Sydney**

The
Keller Plan
Handbook

Fred S. Keller

Professor Emeritus of Psychology,
Columbia University,
and Center for Personalized Instruction,
Georgetown University

J. Gilmour Sherman

Department of Psychology and
Center for Personalized Instruction,
Georgetown University

With a contribution by
Carolina Martuscelli Bori

Department of Psychology
University of São Paulo

RECEIVED

AUG 2 6 1975

MANKATO STATE COLLEGE LIBRARY
MANKATO, MN

Essays on a Personalized System of Instruction

LB 1031
.K39

Copyright © 1974 by W. A. Benjamin, Inc. Philippines copyright 1974 by W. A. Benjamin, Inc.

All rights reserved. No part of this publication may be reproduced, stored in a retrieval system, or transmitted, in any form or by any means, electronic, mechanical, photocopying, recording, or otherwise, without the prior written permission of the publisher. Printed in the United States of America. Published simultaneously in Canada. Library of Congress catalog No. 73-11821.

ISBN 0-8053-5236-8: paperbound edition
ISBN 0-8053-5239-2: clothbound edition
BCDEFGHJ-HA-798765

To B. F. Skinner

375877

 **PREFACE**

We wrote this book primarily for the reader who would like to learn about the *personalized system of instruction*, a new way of teaching that is finding considerable acceptance in the world today. In a set of independently written essays, we have sketched the origins of the system, its basic features, and how it may be put to use by interested instructors. We have also indicated something of its current range of application, its instigation of research, and its grounding in behavior theory. We have suggested some of its limitations and tried to answer questions that are commonly raised about it.

This is not the standard type of *handbook*, in several respects. It isn't based on years of well-established practice or research; PSI is barely ten years old. It doesn't represent a broad consensus of opinion ranging over many fields of study and carefully documented. Its chapters sometimes overlap in content, and differences in terminology may occasionally be found. We may even be in disagreement now and then in connection with some minor point. But with respect to fundamental issues we are in accord and have been since the early days of PSI.

Personalized instruction is the brainchild of our collaboration in 1963 and 1964 with two Brazilian teachers, Rodolpho Azzi and Carolina

Martuscelli Bori. As a method of university instruction it was launched, in almost its present form, at the University of Brasília in 1964. The spread of the system throughout Brazil owes much to the efforts of Dr. Bori, now at the University of São Paulo. In Chapter Seven she brings us up to date on what has happened to it in her country during the past ten years.

The final word on PSI has not been spoken. We hear of fresh adoptions and extensions almost every day. Refinements in the operation of the plan have already been reported and more are sure to follow. Research within the boundaries of the basic format is being carried out in several institutions. By the time this book is in the reader's hands, it will be to some degree outdated. But there will still exist within its pages a prescription which, if followed, may lead to happier and more effective teaching.

Georgetown University   Fred S. Keller
September, 1974   J. Gilmour Sherman

CONTENTS

History of Education

The decent docent doesn't doze;
He teaches standing on his toes.
His student dassn't doze and does,
And that's what teaching is and was.

David McCord, *What Cheer* (1945)

PROLOGUE

You begin with discontent. You have shuffled your pack of cards so many times that every hand is familiar. You have replaced lectures with demonstrations, demonstrations with discussions, discussions with laboratory sessions, laboratory sessions with demonstrations, and demonstrations with lectures. You have added and subtracted, combined and separated, in every conceivable way. You have used movies, tape-recordings, and closed-circuit television; you have changed your textbook every year or used something in its stead. You have even tried teaching machines. You have worked with all types and all frequencies of examination. You have done just about everything, but nothing seems to be much better than it was before, at least for long, and you're about ready to throw in the sponge. You dream of becoming an Associate Dean, or wish you had nothing to do but research.

You recognize your failure. You see it everywhere, every day, in the conduct of your pupils. You find it in the overheard remark, in the sullen aside, the averted gaze, the lame excuse, the half-concealed insult, and the obvious joy at the sound of the bell which ends the classroom hour. But you see it best of all in the distribution of grades at the end of the course. Year after year it is just the same: ten percent of the class, maybe less, completes the course with the standing you desire for all, and just as large a proportion fails. Your students may be more carefully selected, better qualified in background knowledge, and more desirous to learn than ever before, but their grades at the end of the course continue to be distributed in the standard fashion in spite of all the years that you have been teaching.

You no longer attribute your failure to someone else. You stop complaining about the "system" that blocks you, the "administration" that hems you in and cramps your style; you quit suggesting to your pupils that you could change things for the better if "they" would only let you. You no longer lay the blame on overwork, lack of help, the attitude of your chairman, the impossible goals of mass education, the high priorities of writing and research, or the low estate of teaching.

If this is the situation you are in, you are ready for innovation.

Fred S. Keller

CHAPTER ONE

Education:
Lost in the Middle

J. Gilmour Sherman

Three years ago at a summer country fair in a small New England town I bought a book on education published in 1893. In 1904 the book had belonged to a Miss Madge Goodspeed of Enosburg Falls, Vermont. It was her textbook in a "normal course" for teacher training. As a serious student, she had underlined each important point and liberally indulged in margin notes. About her teacher, nicknamed "Horse Jockey," Miss Goodspeed remarked, "He talks a good deal more than we do." At another point she wondered, "Do you suppose he ever runs down?" On the last few blank pages where Miss Goodspeed prepared for the final exam set for June 7, 1905, she set down a summary of the important principles of education. These she listed as regularity, punctuality, neatness, silence, obedience, and accuracy. She was a good student, for her list captures the message of the book, but at the end of the year Miss Goodspeed concluded her studies with the comment, "I should hate to be a teacher."

Madge was not the first person, or the last, to recognize a bad thing when she saw it. This is not to imply that her text was in any way unusual. Quite the contrary. A trip to any secondhand book store will turn up similar textbooks used in teacher education. The stress is on discipline, and perhaps Madge can be forgiven for not wanting to go into the punishment business.

1

Since 1905 evidence of private unhappiness with teaching has surfaced repeatedly to the point of public distress. Whenever the outcry becomes an issue, particularly a political issue, reformers look for something to change. The search for improvement takes different directions depending upon who is doing the looking.

The easiest remedy to suggest is "improve the physical plant." Billions have been spent by a gadget-oriented society to construct new buildings and fill them with the latest instruments and tools of education. Our schools are better lighted, the color schemes more attractive, the architecture less forbidding than before, and chairs are no longer affixed to the floor. Hardware has been stockpiled, audio-visual aids introduced, and new devices invented. But the resulting improvement in learning does not always seem commensurate with the cost. Education is one of many areas where we begin to feel that perhaps all human problems cannot be solved by technology, or at least by a technology of machines. We have received less than was promised and we feel cheated.

There is some tendency in our reaction of disappointment to discredit and abandon hardware. This would probably be as serious a mistake as it was to believe originally that hardware was the answer. As long as humans are doing the learning the *relation* of the student to his tools, not just the improved design of the instruments, is what ultimately determines educational effectiveness. But a relationship is not easy to see. The notion of a contingency, that is, how behavior is related to its consequences, has proved notoriously elusive and has only recently been recognized. Small wonder that educational progress has generally been sought through the refinement of tangible materials.

The search for improvement has also resulted in the development of new texts, new programs, and new curricula. The result of a decade of work by several curriculum study groups has been excellent new course materials, particularly in mathematics, physics, and biology. The finest available talent participated in the writing; the product could hardly be better. But the cries of educational crisis continue.

The teacher has not been neglected in the search for improved education. Efforts to improve teacher training have been sold as a way to bring about educational reform and solve our educational problems. Teacher-training programs teach instructors about the writing of lesson plans, the assessment of intelligence, the stages of maturational development, and even a little about motivation. Some teachers do improve their performance. As in the theater, where actors get better and audiences stay about the same, experienced teachers improve their presentation. They may draw larger crowds, even if they continue to talk a lot. Improved performance from the students does not necessarily follow.

None of this is to argue against the attempt to provide the finest possible environment, the most skillfully written texts, and the best trained teachers. But it is the students who do (or do not do) the learning. It is to them, to their activity, and to how they make contact with these improved resources that we must now turn.

Previously, when attention was directed toward the student it was done to get him to work harder, to have him meet the reckoning of the final exam, and to be one of the few to succeed, preferably with distinction. The recurring theme of alternate approaches can be described variously as force or bribery, coercion or cajoling, fear or enthusiasm, the cane or the carrot. Both approaches have been used without a clear idea of the effects of reward and punishment, much less a respect for a contingent relation between performance and its consequences. Madge's own distaste for teaching resulted from an extreme stress on discipline, a teaching technique that has killed the spirit of all but a few in each generation. How few really able, outstanding men and women our schools produce! When the principles of positive reinforcement are not well understood, punishment is all that is left. Little matter that it does not produce the desired results. We settle for silence and obedience and hardly bother to discuss better goals for education. We are lucky if we get punctuality and neatness!

Punishment has been alternatively extolled as a virtue and branded as a crime. Apparently we cannot teach with it, and we cannot teach without it. Punishment has the advantage that its effects are immediate. This alone is rewarding to teachers trying to affect change while charged with the custodial care of a sizable group. Stern discipline has been given credit for singling out the strong and proving the mettle of the few and has also been used to isolate and justify a select few to lead. But punishment also has other effects, frequently undesirable, and generally not planned. It has broken the will of some, crumbled the confidence of most, and killed the visions of nearly all. This destruction of spirit is a terrible price to pay for the identification of a society's elect and a culture's heroes.

The model is close to that of military basic training which traditionally has been directed toward establishing control, maintaining order, and making the adherence to instructions a primary goal. This is not accomplished without some sacrifice of the individual, his dignity, and his imagination. An educational system designed to tame students can hardly be expected to make them creative at the same time. When punitive systems do lead to inventiveness, the ingenuity engendered is apt to be directed toward devising methods of escape. The dropout rate has been noted, the lack of originality lamented.

Physical punishment is generally being abandoned in our schools. It has been replaced by more subtle and perhaps more cruel disciplinary measures. The inhibiting tyranny of constant judgement, which does not allow the freedom to be wrong without penalty is, in effect, a design for producing anxiety. Denying the right to make one's mistakes in private is humiliating, even dehumanizing. The hurt of public ridicule and loss of self-respect is more vicious than is the sting of the rod. No wonder release from school is almost universally welcomed. No wonder some even take absence without leave.

One modern fact of life, the inevitability of the normal-curve grade distribution, confronts the student from the outset with slim chance of success. The insult of being prejudged "average" quickly humbles all but a few and condemns the humbled to live out their lives viewing themselves as mediocre. A few rebuffed attempts to gain distinction are sufficient to discourage most students and convince them of the justice of this harsh judgement of mediocrity. The struggle is forsaken, the verdict accepted. The job of producing the average has been accomplished almost as if it were intended.

Madge Goodspeed gave us her verdict. Successive generations of students, now parents and voters, record their objections to such a system by voting "No" on school-bond issues. Others write articles and books of protest. But denunciation is of little value without a plan for an alternative.

Some schools have been founded on a plan of more humane procedures. With a slogan that inquiry must not be blunted, permissiveness has become the theme, development of the individual, the goal, and total freedom for the student to choose his own course of study, the method. The catalogues of such institutions stress "meaningful education," "relevance," "involvement," "experimental learning." Some schools have no rules, no requirements, and no curriculum. Self-criticism replaces judgement by the faculty. In the quest for fulfillment and adjustment, punishment has been eliminated.

But merely ending compulsion is not an educational method. Without a theory of behavior there are no general principles to guide the decisions of an educational institution. Without an analysis of the alternative of positive reinforcement, there is little to replace punitive controls. At its worst, the result is a behavioral vacuum where there is no discipline and where rewards are available for the taking without any relation to performance. The product is a happiness born of ignorance. But happiness is not the equivalent of stimulation. There are some reports that these liberated students are not even happy.

From those who see themselves as guardians of the academic tradition the reaction to such experimental institutions has been loud and clear—"restore standards." This plea is almost always a thinly disguised call to reassert discipline and punishment. Excellence at almost any price has some appeal when the alternative is slipshod. Thus we have come full circle without analyzing the issue—the role of punitive controls in the educational system.

What has been lost in the middle of this controversy is, of course, education. The battle of the gentle versus the rigorous becomes the dispute between the liberal "do-gooder" and the "reactionary." The colloquy goes on generating heat and more name calling. Data are collected, articles are written, institutions are founded to demonstrate the superiority of the hard versus the soft approach. Indulging ourselves in the debate of these traditional philosophical and political issues, we have failed to recognize an alternative. As a result our schools are not teaching our children to read, write, and reckon—skills almost everyone could learn well and without undue emotional scars. Our ignorance, or rejection, of a science of behavior has allowed the continuation of an unnecessary argument. If a system of penalties were the only way to produce mastery, the choice might come down to personal preference; a decision about which to avoid—pain or ignorance. The choice then would be between whether it is better to continue to suffer the ravages and waste of punitive systems or to accept the decay of intellectual achievement.

The choice does not have to be made. The confrontation is unnecessary. The debate is a waste. There is an alternative that works.

Continuing the old arguments serves only to delay the time when we get on with the job of designing educational systems on a different model—positive reinforcement. The few who tried in the past did so without a theory of learning to guide them. Learning is too complex a process to be produced successfully on a patchwork, intuitive basis. In 1905 there was no systematic theoretical alternative. Now, however, the development of reinforcement theory provides a system from which we can begin to design educational procedures that are both nonpunitive and effective. That is what this book is about.

CHAPTER TWO

The History of PSI

Fred S. Keller

The teaching plan with which this book concerns itself had its beginnings on an evening in late March, 1963, in front of the fireplace in my Englewood, New Jersey, home. It came at the end of a long brainstorming session in which four psychologists took part: Rodolpho Azzi and Carolina Martuscelli Bori, then at the University of São Paulo, Brazil; J. Gilmour Sherman, who had accompanied them to the United States during his tenure of a Fulbright-Hayes Professorship at their institution; and myself, then still teaching at Columbia University.

All four of us had been invited to the new University of Brasília in the Brazilian capital, to work together in founding a Department of Psychology, with freedom to follow our own dictates and fancies in carrying out the task. My friends had been collecting books, equipment, and ideas in the United States, and now we had reached the point of planning how to teach our introductory course, as well as those courses that followed, when not compelled to do so in the standard way.

The group was *operant* in its orientation—tarred with the brush of *reinforcement theory*. Azzi and Martuscelli Bori had been colleagues

Portions of the present chapter which deal with early tryouts of PSI at Columbia University and at the University of Brasília are rough quotations from a talk delivered in Mexico City on January 24, 1972, at the Second Symposium on Behavior Modification, under auspices of the National Autonomous University of Mexico.

of mine at São Paulo in 1961, and Sherman had worked with me earlier at Columbia. On the evening in question, the three of them had just returned from a trip to Cambridge, Providence, Washington, D.C., and one or two other places, in which they had conferred with such helpful advisors and psychologists as Blough, Boren, Brady, Dews, Ferster, Findley, Herrnstein, Lindsley, Pierrel, Riggs, Schlosberg, Sidman, and Skinner, among others. They were fired with enthusiasm and eager to profit from everything that they had learned.

They were especially excited by what they had heard and seen in Professor Skinner's Natural Science course at Harvard and by the Behavioral Technology course that Charles Ferster was teaching at the Institute for Behavioral Research (I.B.R.), in Silver Spring, Maryland; and we were *all* convinced that traditional teaching methods were sadly out of date. To this may be added the fact that we had been earlier impressed by the teaching-machine and programmed-textbook movement. Azzi had translated Holland and Skinner's *Analysis of Behavior* [1] into Portuguese for Brazilian students; Sherman had bought a machine and worked on a program for it; and I had taught a seminary at Columbia on these techniques of instruction.

The upshot of our give-and-take on that occasion was a plan that I described in my diary that night as a combination of Columbia, Harvard, and I.B.R. procedures, which promised to become "one of the most exciting and most radical [courses] ever given in a university setting." One month later, in my entry for April 29, I was more explicit:

> The Education program . . . represents a distillation of many things: the method of laboratory teaching at Columbia—in Psychology 1-2 and Psychology 127; the method used at I.B.R.; the use of programmed instruction where possible; the treatment of textbooks, lectures, conferences, etc., as *rewards* for passing through various stages of individual study and experimentation; the use of lectures as inspirational rather than truly instructional; the measurement of progress by compilations of things the student has successfully done, rather than by grades on examinations.

By August of 1963, my commitment to the project was so great as to lead me to go on record at the Philadelphia meetings of the American Psychological Association with the report of a course that was little more than a dream.[2] Here are some fragments of that paper:

---

[1] James Holland and B. F. Skinner, *Analysis of Behavior: A Program for Self-Instruction,* New York: McGraw-Hill, 1961.

[2] F. S. Keller, "A Personal Course in Psychology." In *The Control of Behavior,* R. Ulrich, T. Stachnik, and J. Mabry, eds., Glenview, Ill.: Scott, Foresman, 1966, pp. 91-93.

[This] is a course with lectures, demonstrations, discussions, laboratory hours, and homework. The lectures and demonstrations are infrequent and primarily inspirational. Ideally, they are interesting, informative, and memorable—even entertaining. Once the course has started, they are produced at suitable places along the way, but only for those students who have reached a point that guarantees an appreciation of their content. . . . Attendance at either lectures or demonstrations, however, is entirely optional, and no examination is based upon them. . . .

The laboratory itself begins on the second or third day of the course and is its most important feature. . . . The student's daily task begins when he has qualified for it—for example, when he has turned in a report on the preceding day's experiment, answered two or three questions on the last reading assignment, studied a description of his laboratory mission for the day, or done all of these things.

. . . When a laboratory task has been completed (and *only* then), the student receives the assignment that will prepare him for the next. . . . It may include textbook study, plain or programmed; the reading of an article or technical report, carefully edited or supplemented to make it fully clear, and provided with a few key questions like those he may be asked at the beginning of the next laboratory session; and other readings may be given solely as a reward for work completed and to whet the appetite for more. . . .

The assistant's functions . . . are very important. He is the one who prepares and checks equipment, collects reports, passes out work assignments, and records, in each student's individual logbook, each important step along the route—including the time of arrival and number of setbacks, if any, before reaching port. He will also collect any student complaints, comments, or suggestions (in writing), which he then passes on to the course director. . . .

The teachers, in a course like this, are not as conspicuous as they were under the old order. . . . They are the ones who design, in every minute detail, and initially for just one student, each day's teaching program; and they are the ones who redesign the program in the light of student performance and assistant's reports. . . . Their general loss in visibility to their students, which might be aversive to longtime performers on the classroom stage, is perhaps offset by the improved reception of their messages when given and, more generally, the increased status of their academic position.

When all the course requirements have been met . . . the student's logbook is examined by the course director, who records the achievement, places the book in the department files, and takes a few moments, perhaps, to offer his congratulations. No final examination is given, no course grade, no reward for speed of attainment, and no punishment for delay. Examining and teaching were inseparable parts of the same educational process, and something better than a letter or a number grade is available in a list of the goals that were reached and the time it took to reach them. The student is ready for Course No. 2, a new logbook, a new cubicle, a new assistant, a new body of fact and skills, and, probably, a new teacher. . . .

Nearly ten years later, I am amazed at the similarity of this imagined course to the one that was actually taught in Brasília, as well as the lack of really basic change that has been made in the format since that time. The daily *modus operandi* was slightly altered, the emphasis on laboratory work decreased, the *proctor* was added to our staff, and we did not rid ourselves of final examinations and letter grades entirely; but the self-pacing feature, the performance requirement for advance, the role of the lecture, and the general spirit of the course remain the same.

When our decision had been made in Englewood, my colleagues went back to Brazil to get ready for the move from São Paulo to Brasília in early 1964—to prepare equipment for the laboratory and work out other details. I used my final term at Columbia to send up a trial balloon. With the aid of a graduate assistant (Lanny Fields) and five seniors in the College, I constructed a miniature course of study along the lines we had proposed.

In the Christmas recess of 1963, this course was offered to three students—two highschool seniors and a college freshman—in the College laboratory. Built around five laboratory exercises, this course was programmed in every tiny detail with respect to equipment, procedures, and reading assignments. I talked to my little class but once, on the first day of the course, and my assistant's interaction with the students was limited almost entirely to testing and handing out assignments as each part of the course was completed. More than any other course I have taught, this one ran itself.

My three young guinea pigs were positive, even enthusiastic, in their reactions to the course. They worked efficiently on their own, progressing at slightly different speeds, and they were all "graduated" within the vacation period. Their single complaint, which was not very loud and which I was too busy to hear, concerned the lack of opportunity for discussion—they wanted someone with whom to talk about their work.

Two months later I joined my colleagues in São Paulo, but before we could move on to Brasília the country underwent a governmental change. The result, for our project, was to delay the inauguration of our first course at Brasília for several months. This meant, in turn, that both Dr. Sherman and I were back in the States before it actually began. I had retired from Columbia and we had both accepted positions at Arizona State University when Rodolpho Azzi, aided by Dr. Martuscelli Bori (our Departmental Coordinator), quietly and efficiently got the project off the ground (See Chapter Seven).

A full account of this first course was never published, although a preliminary sketch appeared at approximately the time when it began.[3] Sixty students were enrolled, many of whom were slated for a psychological career. It was a systematic course, an introduction to reinforcement theory. Each student moved through the course at his own pace through forty-nine units of work, including ten experiments which came early in the year. This experimental work was evaluated by several laboratory assistants, most of them experienced beyond the fourth year of university study. *Reading checks* (Azzi disliked *tests*) were looked after by a Departmental clerk, *Senhor* Daniel, who had no knowledge of psychology and simply checked the students' answers against a master sheet. Nine lectures and sixteen demonstrations, none of which counted as steps in the program, were provided during the year as "reinforcements."

As originally set up, this introduction to the analysis of behavior was composed of three main parts, each of which, in deference to tradition, was to extend for approximately a standard university term. *Part One* was to deal with animal-experimental origins of basic concepts; *Part Two* was to focus on similar fundamentals, but to emphasize *human* conduct; and *Part Three* was to introduce the student to such areas as clinical, educational, industrial, and social psychology.

Only the first two parts were carried through, however, before a University crisis brought the entire curriculum to its end. Part One was twice presented in this period with very good results, both from a student and a faculty point of view. An appreciable number of students dropped out early in the course and an equal number required more than one semester to complete the program. When asked about the course's most desirable feature, the students usually said *self-pacing,* which encouraged a "more responsible" way of study. The least desirable feature reported was the lack of opportunity to discuss the course materials with someone better qualified than *Senhor* Daniel. All of the students who completed the course wrote that, given the option, they would prefer to go on within this format.

Except for Rodolpho Azzi, who eventually gave up teaching, the members of the Brasília staff moved on in 1965 to other positions, in different institutions. What the outcome would have been if they had remained together and the program had been continued can only be surmised. Our original aim had been to let one course of study lead naturally into another, without delay, in accordance with each student's readiness and desire, from the beginning to the end of his psychological training. Had this been allowed to occur, these students might have been the first to show the way, by their example, to freeing higher education from the calendar and the clock.

---

[3] F. S. Keller, C. M. Bori, and R. Azzi, "Um Curso Moderno de Psicologia." *Ciencia ê Cultura* 16 (1964) 307-309.

In describing the two initial tryouts of our plan, I have noted a source of dissatisfaction—there was little or no provision for students to talk with the staff about the subject matter of their study. The remedy for this came as an unexpected bonus from a *second* attempt to set up our procedure in a university classroom setting; it came as a side-effect of using *student proctors* as regular aids in the testing-grading process; and it remains today as an integral (and perhaps the most important) element of the system. To this we shall return in Chapter Two.

Before we leave the present theme, however, another sort of history should be mentioned. Something must be said about anticipations of our system by our predecessors—about practices which antedate our own and bear a close resemblance to them.

To the best of my knowledge, the earliest use of students in the teaching of other students within a schoolroom situation was in the sixteenth century. Jesuit teachers of that period had student *decurions,* each one in charge of ten other students. These decurions listened to recitations, collected papers, kept records, and carried out other duties related to instruction. [4] They exercised in some degree the functions of our *proctors.*

Nearly three hundred years later, at the turn of the nineteenth century, young students were used with some success in the "mutual-tuition" and "monitorial" systems that were made famous by Andrew Bell (1753-1832) and Joseph Lancaster (1778-1838), as well as in the "pupil-teacher" system that replaced them. [5] *Monitors* served, like decurions, to reduce the teacher's burdens and increase the number of students taught.

The go-at-your-own-pace feature of our system has often been used before, even on a large scale, as in military training centers. Here too progress is often stepwise and perfection of performance may be called for. Teaching with lectures is an obvious feature of correspondence-school instruction. And so on. There is probably no single aspect of our system that is really new.

> Even in its totality [I quote from an earlier report][6], the method has been anticipated. This I discovered with some surprise in a recent book by Washburn and Marland, concerning the so-called Winnetka Plan. [7]

[4] Luella Cole, *A History of Education—Socrates to Montessori.* New York: Reinhart & Co., 1950, xi, 700 pp., (see pp. 319-320).

[5] Ibid., pp. 607-609.

[6] F. S. Keller, "Neglected Rewards in the Educational Process." *Proceedings of the 23rd American Conference of Academic Deans,* Los Angeles, 1967, pp. 9-22.

[7] C. W. Washburn, and S. P. Marland, Jr. *Winnetka: The History and Significance of an Educational Experiment.* New York: Prentice-Hall, 1963.

In this book, the story is told of an experiment conducted more than fifty years ago at the San Francisco State Normal School, under the presidency of Dr. Frederick Burk. . . . The parallel with our own method is so striking that I am going . . . to describe the study here.

Students at this normal school [now San Francisco State University] began their practice teaching soon after they arrived, working under the surveillance of supervisors in the different areas of elementary instruction. Two practice teachers were assigned to each class of twenty children. Each supervisor had four such classes, with two practice teachers in each.

One of the supervisors was Mary Ward, a teacher of arithmetic. During a discussion with her practice teachers, one day after class, it was pointed out that the study materials then in use were too hard for some children and too easy for others. Miss Ward suggested that they prepare materials suited to each of three groups—the slow, the average, and the fast. This was done, and the situation improved, but it was soon discovered that, within each group, there were still important differences. "The slower children had different degrees of retardation, the faster ones different degrees of acceleration, and the 'average' spread from almost retarded to almost accelerated."

Before long, Miss Ward and her practice teachers were preparing materials for each individual child. It appeared that, if these materials were suitable for one child, every other child could use them, although at different times. The result, by the end of the year, was a wide range of achievement within the group. The fastest child had done two years' work—twice as much as the slowest child.

Miss Ward reported her findings to Dr. Burk, who immediately "caught fire." He had her describe her experiment to the faculty and he proposed that every supervisor should prepare comparable study materials for his own subject and classes. If written simply and clearly enough, each child could almost "teach himself" with such materials, although the student teacher could always be on hand to help when needed. The proposal was accepted and the supervisors, with their student teachers, began the preparation of "self-instruction bulletins."

These "bulletins" were used at first in conjunction with the teachers' textbooks. They specified the material to be studied, they amplified and clarified where necessary, and they sometimes included supplementary materials. They were given to the classes in mimeographed form and, after one year's tryout, were subjected to revision on the basis of student reaction. In time, they became the only course materials and were even adopted for use in other schools.

From then on, instruction in elementary classes at this normal school was conducted on an individual basis. Each child moved at his own pace, neither hurried nor delayed by other children. Also, the idea spread . . . , in this country and abroad. Perhaps it spread too rapidly and with too little understanding of the essential features, or combination of features, that made it effective.

The amazing similarity of Mary Ward's procedure to that with which we deal in Chapter Three alerts us to the problem of priority and hints at the possibility of other independent formulations (see Chapter Nine).

CHAPTER THREE

The Basic System

Fred S. Keller

In the spring of 1965 at Arizona State University, two variations of the Brasília plan were used in teaching an introductory course in the principles of behavior. In one of these courses, ten student aides, called *proctors*, replaced *Senhor* Daniel in grading and discussing unit tests for a class of ninety-four students. In the other, involving fewer students, these functions were performed by the instructor himself, with the help of his graduate teaching assistant.[1]

Both courses were deemed successful enough to warrant further exploration of our method, and in the ensuing semesters they went through several stages of more or less independent development in the hands of each instructor. Although the following account deals with the course arrived at by Keller, it represents in some degree the pooled experience of both teachers. The system that resulted from our efforts is essentially the system that we would support today. It is what we

---

[1]The proctored course was taught by F. S. Keller, aided by his graduate teaching assistant, Susan Anderson; the other course was taught by J. G. Sherman, with the assistance of Paul Wittenburg.

mean by a *personalized, proctorial,* or *programmed system of instruction* (PSI).[2]

Imagine for a moment that you are once again a college freshman. Assume that you have just arrived, along with about one hundred other students, at the first meeting of a course in elementary psychology with laboratory. This is a one-term course, with seventy-five-minute class meetings scheduled for Tuesday and Thursday mornings. (Wednesday afternoon and Saturday morning periods will soon be added in response to student demand.) Since this is the first meeting of the class, you probably arrived late and missed some of the professor's opening remarks, but an assistant greets you pleasantly and gives you a mimeographed handout, which reads in part as follows:

> This is a course through which you may move, from start to finish, at your own pace. You will not be held back by other students or forced to go ahead before you are ready. At best you may meet all the course requirements in less than one semester; at worst you may not complete the job within that time. How fast you go is up to you.
> The work of this course will be divided into thirty units of content, which correspond roughly to a series of twenty homework assignments and ten laboratory exercises. These units will come in numerical order, and you must show your mastery of each by passing a "readiness test" or carrying out an experiment, before moving on to the next.
> A good share of your *reading* for this course may be done in the classroom, at those times when no lectures, demonstrations, or other activities are taking place. The classroom, that is, will sometimes be a study hall.
> The lectures and demonstrations in this course will have a different relation to the rest of your work than is usually the rule. They will be provided only when you have demonstrated your readiness to appreciate them; no examination will be based upon them; and you need not attend them if you do not wish. When a certain percentage of the class has reached a given point in the course, a lecture or a demonstration will be available at a stated time, but it will not be compulsory.
> The teaching staff of your course will include proctors, assistants, and an instructor. A *proctor* is an undergraduate who has been chosen for his

---

[2]This account is based on a report, written by the author while he was a Visiting Scientist at the Institute for Behavioral Research, Silver Spring, Md., in 1968. It was later presented, with minor changes, as an address to the 1968 Autumn Conference of the Pacific Northwest Association for College Physics, in Seattle, and published under the title, *A Programmed System of Instruction,* in an *Educational Technology Monograph* prepared by the Kalamazoo Valley Intermediate School District, of Kalamazoo, Michigan, in 1969.

mastery of the course content and orientation, for his maturity of judgment, for his understanding of the special problems that confront you as a beginner, and for his willingness to assist. It is he who will pass upon your readiness tests as satisfactory or unsatisfactory. His decision will ordinarily be law, but if he is ever in serious doubt, he can appeal to the classroom assistant, or even the instructor, for a ruling. Failure to pass a test on the first try, the second, the third, or even later, will not be held against you. It is better that you get too much testing than not enough, if your final success in the course is to be assured.

Your work in the laboratory will be carried out under the direct supervision of a laboratory assistant, whose detailed duties cannot be listed here. . . . There will also be a graduate classroom assistant upon whom your proctor will depend for various materials (assignments, study questions, special readings, and so on), and who will keep up to date all progress records for course members. The classroom assistant will confer with the instructor daily, aid the proctors on occasion, and act in a variety of ways to further the smooth operation of the course machinery.

The instructor will have as his principal responsibilities: (a) the selection of all study material used in the course; (b) the organization and mode of presenting this material; (c) the construction of tests and examinations; and (d) the final evaluation of each student's progress. It will be his duty also to provide lectures, demonstrations, and discussion opportunities for all students who have earned the privilege; to act as a clearing-house for requests and complaints; and to arbitrate in any case of disagreement between students and proctors or assistants. . . .

All students in the course are expected to take a final examination, in which the entire term's work will be represented. With certain exceptions, this examination will come at the same time for all students — at the end of the term. . . . The examination will consist, in part, of questions which you have already answered on the readiness tests. Twenty-five percent of your course grade will be based on this examination; the remaining seventy-five percent will be based on the number of units of reading and laboratory work that you have successfully completed during the term.

Together with this description and a few items of information concerning course operation, staffing, and study materials, you are handed your first work unit — your first assignment — and listen to a few inspiring words from your instructor. He outlines the rules once more for those who didn't read them or didn't believe them; he expresses his complete faith in your maturity and your willingness to work for what you get; he promises you a square deal; he tells you of his great expectations; and he ends by suggesting that you drop the course at once if the prospects don't appeal.

Along with the unit assignment, you receive a set of *study questions* and some advice on how to use them. These questions may vary in their number and generality, in accordance with the type of reading that they cover, but they are designed to include every point that your instructor thinks essential in the reading assignment (and to exclude, perhaps, some item that he believes to be of lesser merit).

You are now on your own in the course, although you may not realize it. You are somewhat disturbed by your freedom, by the amount of testing that you see ahead, by the talk about "excellence" and "perfection," by the absence of lectures with which to clarify your reading, and by the general strangeness of everything. On the other hand, there are the positive features: noncompulsory lecture attendance, going at your own speed, and getting your first A. You decide to hang on, at least until the deadline date for dropping out.

The course description tells you exactly what steps to take from this day on. First, you are to study your assignment until it is fully mastered—until you are sure that you can cope successfully with all the study questions of the unit. You can do this work at home, in your dormitory, or in the classroom (which the instructor recommended). Other students will be studying in the classroom, and the study-hall proctor or the assistant will always be on hand to help you if you have trouble with any part of the assignment. Besides, the study hall will be the source of announcements and new materials for the course. Perhaps you decide to work at home.

When you are ready for testing, you report to your study-hall proctor or the assistant, who doesn't seem surprised to see you and doesn't ask where you have been. He sends you immediately to the testing room, or area, or asks you to wait a moment until a place is ready.[3] When you get to the testing proctor, you receive one of the four or more test forms for the unit on which you have been working. The proctor also hands you your examination booklet on one or two of the pages of which you are to answer your test questions.[4]

In ten or fifteen minutes, when you have completed your answers, you return your test form to the testing proctor. He records the event and sends you, with your test booklet, into the room next door for grading. There you find, in a special cubicle or at a special table, the

---

[3] The number of students to be tested at one time will depend upon the current availability of proctors for grading, and a pile-up of students waiting to be tested is preferrable to a pile-up waiting to be graded.

[4] Sherman used a special answer sheet for every test, rather than a "blue book," but each method has its merits. A booklet permits an occasional interaction between the student and his instructor or the assistant, by way of written comment, query, or reply; but "test insulation" is probably greater with the answer sheet.

grading proctor to whom you have been assigned for the duration of the course, and to whom you will always report except on those occasions when a substitute is necessary.

The next step is the important one. The proctor, with you beside him, grades your readiness test. First he scans the test quickly, check-marking each wrong answer with his pen. If he finds too many, the grading operation stops right there and you are advised to study further before coming to be tested and graded; *this* test, your proctor tells you, will not be counted. You are also told not to come back until a certain time has elapsed—say thirty minutes. This is not only to encourage studying, but to keep you from "shopping around" for the test that you like, or from gaining familiarity with all the available questions.

However, if you have made but two or three errors, you are given a chance to defend your answers. If your defense is convincing, and if a restatement of the questions by the proctor evokes satisfactory replies, he adds an *OK* to his earlier check marks to indicate a change of grade. If your defense is judged to be inadequate, he discusses the matter with you, recommends restudy of certain material, and sends you away with the promise that your failure will not weigh against you, either then or in the future.

In case all your answers are initially correct or get an *OK*, your proctor probably congratulates you, records your success, and sends you back to the study hall for your next assignment. If time permits, he may ask you why you answered one or two questions as you did, in order to probe the depth of your understanding or just to get acquainted. He keeps your test booklet when you leave and will pass it along to the assistant or to the instructor at the end of the period, for inspection and further recording.

This sequence of events will be repeated for the remaining units of the course, with review assignments and laboratory exercises introduced along the way. The number of tests that you may need to take on each work unit may vary considerably, but the average will probably be a little less than two. When the last test has been passed, you can arrange the date of your final examination, if one is to be given. Beyond that, you are free to turn to other matters or, ideally, begin another course of study under a similar program of advancement.

This learning situation is in some respects similar to those one meets in the area of programmed textbooks, teaching machines, and computer-based instruction.[5] There is an initial analysis and organiza-

---

[5]When we first described our system of teaching to our colleagues at Arizona State University, one faculty member asked: "Isn't your method like programmed instruction?" When I replied that in some ways it was, he said, "Then I don't like it!"

tion of subject matter; there is specification of objectives; there is a provision for individualized progression, as each basic step is mastered; and there is feedback to the instructor which enables him to improve his program.

In the case of PSI, however, the steps of the program are not *frames* in a *set;* they are more inclusive and can better be described as "reading assignments" or "laboratory exercises." The response is not the completion of a frame, but is the resultant, one might say, of many such completions, better desecribed as the understanding of a principle, a concept, a technique, or the solution of a problem. Advance within the program is not based simply upon the appearance of a confirming word or the presentation of the next frame but follows personal approval of a larger sample of behavior.

The use of a programmed text, a teaching machine, closed-circuit television, or a computer is possible under PSI. It may even be desirable at times. But such devices are not to be equated with the system itself.

Relatively minor roles are given in our plan to the lecture and the demonstration. Their purpose is primarily motivational. They are not central to the educational process and they could be eliminated entirely without serious damage. Yet they are not useless. They permit an instructor to appear at his inspirational best before an unusually receptive and well-prepared audience. He is free to speak about some favorite topic, some newly discovered fact, some experiment in which he is engaged, or almost anything he wishes, without feeling that he should be doing something more useful or significant. Also, lectures and demonstrations let the students see their instructor in action, to sample his style, to get the flavor of his thinking, under the best of circumstances. No threat of future quizzing hangs over their heads, nothing important rides on their failure to catch the detail of his message, and no struggle with note taking distracts them from the flow of words or significance of the events to which they are attending.

By ordinary standards, lectures and demonstrations, within a course like this, are of short duration (perhaps twenty or thirty minutes) and small number (no more than eight or ten in a semester). If a lecture or a demonstration, no matter how interesting, competes with an opportunity to pass a test, or even to prepare for one, it will attract no more than a handful of those who have earned the right to come. If a lecture is announced in advance, with a catchy title, it may encourage a flurry of test taking to qualify for the event, which may then go unattended. By increasing the available hours per week in which tests can be taken and graded, by placing a ban on testing and grading while the speech or demonstration is in progress, and by making each performance as interesting as he can, an instructor may attract a modest crowd. He will soon discover, however, that other features of the course are more important and that the lecture or the show is vastly overrated.

Optimally, in a course like ours, every student should come out with an *A*. In practice, however, this is seldom the case. Some students may have failed to withdraw from the course when they should have; others may have done insufficient reviewing for a final examination, thus bringing their course grade down to a *B*; and a less-than-*A* grade may be given to the student who has not passed all his course units within the term but cannot make use of the *Incomplete*.

(There are many reasons why a student's work in any course of study may be interrupted. *Illness* has traditionally been a good one, and *outside work* has been grudgingly accepted on occasion. But there are others that deserve to be recognized in any school which pretends to an awareness of the individual needs of its students, or which sponsors activities that conflict with full-time devotion to study. Extracurricular activities of one kind or another—glee club, dramatics, publications, athletics, recognized social functions, even the demands of married life and other personal-social matters—these should also be considered. A student under PSI can often recover from such interruptions with a little extra effort when the critical season has passed, but sometimes he may still be in arrears when the term comes to its end. He must then accept a final grade that represents neither his ability nor his motivation, or he must be given an *Incomplete*. Until the day when letters and numbers are no longer used as they are now, and when a course of study is terminated whenever its requirements are met, the *Incomplete* has value. Without it there can be no true self-pacing; properly administered it need not be abused; and the bookkeeping problems it may generate should not stand in its way.)

Ours is an interlocking system of instruction. Each person involved gets his rewards from the behavior of the others. Each one's work produces the task for the next in line. The student provides work for the proctor; the proctor *and* the student give the assistant his data; the assistant provides the instructor with proctor and student feedback; and the instructor starts the cycle all over again. Each one gets maximal satisfaction when the other one's work is well done. It is a system of *mutual reinforcement*; and no teaching system can be called a good one unless it is just that.

The proctor is the new link in this chain. His principal job is that of decreasing the gap of understanding between the student and the teacher—a gap that is sometimes very wide. He can do this because he has a repertory of behavior that is intermediate between the two with respect to the subject matter of the course. He may find logic in an answer that an instructor would never have perceived; he may restate a question in a way that brings out evidence of knowledge; and he may, by example or parallel statement, strengthen a student's grasp of a concept. He provides the individual consideration that a student may never have had before.

He is not a teacher or a coach, in the traditional sense of these terms. He should not give lectures, nor should he attempt to drill his students in the "one right answer." But he may check on test responses that clearly hit, or miss, the target; he may raise objections to other answers and evaluate their defense (an evaluation which will in turn be evaluated by the assistant or the instructor); he may clarify points on which he is well informed; and he may direct his students to certain readings or to consultation with staff members.

He is helped in his work by (1) his experience with a similar course in which he was recently successful; (2) a weekly proctors' meeting in which every question on every test may be discussed, together with related matters; (3) a handy list of acceptable answers to these questions, to jog his memory if needed (he may sometimes have to cover two-thirds of a course within a grading period); and, usually, (4) relevant knowledge from advanced courses within the same subject-matter field.

The above refers to the *grading* proctors, ten or more of whom would be required for a class of one hundred students. There may also be a *testing* proctor and a *study-hall* proctor. The former is really not a proctor, in the sense of furthering instruction. He does all the testing for each unit and keeps a record for each student. His work could be done by a reliable clerk with a grade-school education. If no such clerk is to be had, grading proctors may take their turn as testing proctors in regular rotation, each carrying a portion of this noneducational load.

The study-hall proctor is important, so much that the position may be filled by the instructor or his assistant. He is the one who stands between the *textbook* and the student, in the same way that the grading proctor stands between the student and the instructor. He clarifies obscure passages, helps with difficult operations, explains unintelligible references, and the like. His work load will depend upon the adequacy of the textbook and the study questions, but it will not be overwhelming. He generally serves a small percentage of the class, usually its weakest members, and the number of cries for help will decrease as study habits are improved and the students gain in self-reliance.

The study-hall proctor may be selected on the basis of his course history, achievement, or special aptitude for the task. Or he may be drawn from the grading group in regular rotation, regardless of special qualifications. The first procedure would seem to be better, but we do not know for certain. The study-hall proctor who acts too much like a teacher in his tendencies to talk, to clarify, "to help," is not necessarily the most effective promotor of learning in the classroom.

The work of the *classroom assistant*[6] is subject to considerable variation. Early in the course, when the instructor is developing his materials and organization, he may do no more than minor chores. Once the course is under way, however, his duties could include the distribution of assignments, study questions, and other material to the proctors, the regulation of student flow from place to place, the checking of supplies, the maintenance of progress charts, and helping out in demonstrations or in proctors' meetings.

Still later, if given some clerical aid, the classroom assistant may preside at proctors' meetings, evaluate proctors' ratings, prepare demonstrations, or give an occasional lecture. He may become practically indistinguishable at times from the teacher of the course. This is as it should be, in terms of his own growth and the instructor's need for time in which to change the content of the course, but it should never be permitted unless the assistant fully understands the system of rewards upon which the course's success depends. The classical role of the assistant as a boss or martinet is out of place within a course like this one. The whip is never needed; motivation grows by itself with every unit passed, even for the slower-moving students, and additional pressure would only be disruptive.

Some final comment should be made about the *instructor* as a manager of learning. He is the member of the system, as already noted, who selects and analyzes the material to be mastered, who decides on how to present it, who constructs the various questions based upon it, and who arranges the *conditions of reward* (see Chapter Five) essential to effective education for his pupils.

The textbook must be carefully read before it is selected, to determine its suitability for students who will be questioned upon it in detail and who will be given a chance to defend their answers. Errors, confusions, and contradictions that might be unnoticed or unremarked within a conventional system will stand out as unsightly blemishes under PSI. Study questions must skirt them, proctors must be schooled to deal with them, test questions must take them into account, and supplements may have to be provided to avoid the damage they might do.

Analysis of course material into study units is another task for the instructor. The textbook chapters may not be of suitable size, and

---

[6]Within the context of this chapter, the *classroom assistant* is distinguished from the *laboratory assistant*, whose functions are not considered here. The classroom assistant is roughly comparable to the *course manager*, as described by Dr. Sherman in Chapter Four. He is ordinarily a graduate student (a *TA*), but an advanced undergraduate might exercise some of his functions on occasion.

mastery of their content has never before been asked of all his pupils. The amount of material assigned may have less than a direct relation to the amount that a student learns. The difficulty of a unit can only be estimated roughly, in advance of an actual tryout, and the instructor of such a course may be in for some surprises.

In writing study questions, the instructor must avoid the extremes of over-generality and over-specificity. If his questions are too detailed, they may delay the grasp of major concepts and broad principles—the student won't see the woods for the trees. If too general, the questions will foster confusion and will restrict the number and variety of test questions that can be based upon them.

Test questions are harder to compose than study questions. Ideally, the forms for a single unit should be clearly different from each other, but should sample all the basic parts of the assignment. They should minimize the role of guessing, and they should be suitable for proctors' grading without encouraging drill in single verbal responses. Wherever possible they should encourage concept formation, thinking, and reference to affairs that lie beyond the purely academic.

Finally, the instructor in such a course has feedback data on every question he constructs and everything he writes. As a result, many test questions will have to be rewritten or discarded, study questions will have to be revised, and supplements to his reading assignments may have to be composed. If this supplementation is on a large enough scale, it may give him a chance to develop original assignments, testing them out on his students as he goes along. Unit by unit, little by little, he may write a text of his own, as part of his daily teaching function, rather than at times which might better be devoted to research or recreation.

CHAPTER FOUR

Logistics

J. Gilmour Sherman

Pre-Logistics: "Givens" of the System

PSI has usually been associated with five defining characteristics: (1) mastery learning, (2) self-pacing, (3) a stress on the written word, (4) student proctors, and (5) the use of lectures to motivate rather than to supply essential information. Each feature has some natural corollaries.

A *mastery requirement* means just that—a demand for perfection. Accomplishment can only be detected from performance. The student must be called upon to respond frequently, and his activities must have consequences. It follows naturally then that there must be repeated testing and errors should result in a program of remediation rather than a system of penalties. Equally important, success must be rewarded. Grades must reflect final accomplishments, not the number of errors made along the way, and grading standards must be absolute rather than competitive and comparative.

Given a mastery requirement with the above implications, the second characteristic, a go-at-your-own-pace feature, is mandatory. Excellence cannot be commanded on schedule. Individual differences cannot be denied. No humane approach would advocate that they be eliminated. Since we must allow either achievement or speed to vary, the requirement of excellence implies *self-pacing*. Most traditional educational practices are the result of a decision to hold time constant, and this produces the grade distribution normally found. It was exactly to provide an alternative to that result that led to the development of PSI. Self-pacing is an essential feature of the method.

The last three features follow directly from the first two. Once self-pacing is allowed, it will occur and be incompatible with a lock-step lecture approach. *Written materials* (or audio-visual media where available and economically justifiable) must become the major informational source. This heavy reliance on the written word requires that the materials be presented more clearly than ever before, with objectives clearly specified, and sequenced in small steps leading from the simple to the more complex. New information must be presented only when the student is prepared to deal successfully with new concepts. All this implies a re-examination of course content. Not without some pain, the teacher must ask himself what is worth teaching since now he knows that what is taught will be learned.

Given a number of students who are engaged in repetitive testing, working at different speeds, and dealing with a wide range of material at any point in time, we must find a means to supplement and amplify the instructor. The *proctor* or tutor becomes an essential feature of the system who not only copes with this new kind of diversity, but also allows the teacher to devote more of his time to those individuals and problems that require his level of expertise. Traditional teaching squanders society's investment in the education of the expert. The professor is too valuable to be assigned a large repetitive job that can be delegated to others, especially when others can do it as well, if not better. The proctor, who provides nearly limitless individual attention to the student, also benefits through learning by teaching, and allows the teacher's time to be used when really needed. The proctor is not only an essential feature but perhaps the most valuable contribution of PSI.

Finally, the function of *lectures,* as indicated above, is dramatically different. Since they are no longer required, this means for most of us they need to be better. As lecturing is no longer the teacher's major commitment he must now learn new roles as a creator of materials and a manager of a learning system. He also must learn to meet individual students on those occasions when they need his expertise. He has already given his stock of ready answers to his proctors. In this interlocking system, not only the student, but also the teacher must be creative, imaginative, and must earn his *A*. It is dangerous, exciting, and challenging, but teachers should not settle for less.

Areas of Decision

Because the above sets forth a discussion of the essentials of PSI, it is phrased in the imperative. An individual's views on the merits of these defining characteristics and their implications determine his decision whether or not to adopt this teaching method. The essentials are the givens of the system and outline broadly the procedures of any PSI course. The details of implementation within those guidelines are another matter; they are not prescribed, and choices have to be made. The details of the system are the subject of the remainder of this chapter.

The Logistics: Crucial Details

The word "details" may be found in the thesaurus under the category "unimportance," along with such words as "petty," "paltry," "minutiae," and "insignificance." As PSI changes the role of the student and the teacher, it also changes the importance of what might be thought of as trivial in a traditional context. If this chapter makes no other point it should make clear that attention to detail can make the difference between success and failure in a PSI course.

Within the guidelines of the defining characteristics, logistical decisions call for choosing from a wide range of alternatives. Generally the question is not what is "right," or "wrong," or even in many cases what is "best." Sometimes local considerations of subject matter, student background, university policy, or even the physical space of the classroom will determine a choice. In many cases there are both benefits and liabilities attached to each alternative. In the absence of necessity, it becomes a matter of the individual teacher's preference and style as to what to gain and what to lose. The important points to be recognized by anyone about to design a PSI course are that there are alternatives, that the decisions made will influence the behavior of everyone in the system (students, proctors, course manager, and professor), and that the only fatal error is not to decide. One hundred students wandering around with incomplete instructions, not knowing what to do, when, where, and with whom, produces a confusion that is worse than the effects of even the most unfortunate logistical decision. In a PSI course, the details are critical.

The logistics of the system can be considered under three headings: materials, course policy, and implementation.

I. Materials

Normally, PSI courses are based upon a standard textbook, journal articles, other readings, or some form of traditional printed material. Unless specifically designed for individualized instruction, these materials cannot stand alone and must be supplemented by a study guide.

The study guide breaks the course into units. Each unit guide consists of an introduction, statement of objectives, procedure, study questions, and such supplementary material as may be dictated by the specific course content. There must be tests for each unit and proctor materials to aid the proctor in "grading."

The major decisions to be made are:

1. *Number of units* for a semester (a quarter or a year) course. There is no magic answer as to the right number of units. As the number of units approaches the number of class testing days, self-pacing disappears. The Tuesday-Thursday class working over a fifteen-week semester would call for something less than thirty units. At the other extreme, as the number of units approaches only one or two, the course begins to look much like a normal course with a midterm and final! It is probably wise to provide the opportunity for the student to check in about once a week. For a fifteen-week semester, eighteen units has proved to be a popular choice. Any number of units between fifteen and twenty seems to work equally well and describes what we might think of as the normal range. A class schedule that provides more frequent testing opportunities makes it reasonable to slightly increase the number of units assigned. It is probably better to err on the side of too many units than too few. On the other hand, for any given number of students, more proctors are required as testing becomes more frequent.

2. *Unit size*. Again there is no formula. The nature of the material in a few disciplines may dictate unit size and test length. A unit usually covers about a week's work. An average unit size can be arrived at indirectly. Unit tests should normally require fifteen-twenty minutes to answer and about five minutes to correct. Longer tests tend to be avoided, encouraging procrastination. Tests which take more time to correct and discuss produce waiting lines unless there is a large number of proctors. The tests are designed to quiz the student on every major unit objective and should not merely sample and thus estimate what has been learned. This limits the unit size to an informational content that can be fully tested in fifteen-twenty minutes. Units are too long when one must resort to sampling, or dramatically extending the test time in order to be comprehensive. While this rule-of-thumb is indirect and approximate, it is better than a decision rule based on some fixed number of pages, or alternatively, taking chapters as they are in most textbooks and making a unit equal a chapter.

3. *Unit sequence*. Given the above considerations concerning *average* unit size, other factors suggest sequential arrangements that deviate

from something approximating "equal difficulty" units.[1] The first few units should produce a high success rate, which generally means these units are both shorter and conceptually more simple than later ones. A good running start with a few successes can avoid a lot of problems later on. Similar considerations may suggest deviations from uniformity at other points within the program.

When the course is by nature cumulative, the sequence may appear to be determined by course content. In some cases, this apparently simple solution may need examination. Some students will not finish the course if self-pacing is confined within semester limits. Where the self-paced feature is not extended by a liberal *Incomplete* policy a few students will never see the last few units. Where it is important that students touch base with every topic, and where advanced courses require some familiarity with specific introductory material, some care must be given to what information is included in those last units. This may mean covering all the more important concepts early, or organizing the material in a repeat spiral. The latter procedure of presenting each important topic twice, once in a preliminary form in the early units and again in more detail in the last half of the sequence, is not always easy to arrange, but if possible it can avoid the problem of some students progressing to later courses with no knowledge at all in some areas.

Where the course is apparently noncumulative, unit sequence may seem irrelevant. There even may be courses where it is sound practice to allow students to take units in any order they choose. This is probably less frequently the case than one might guess. It is a rare topic that does not involve some progressive development. The subject matter analysis involved in writing PSI materials may reveal a cumulative feature not previously recognized. A fixed sequence also provides for planned review.

4. Review units. The fact that course content is broken into units does not imply that the end result must be a fragmented view of the subject matter. Study guides (see below) can provide integration. Some form of planned review can emphasize relationships across units as well as provide the occasion for refreshing and maintaining earlier material. There are two review procedures that have proved most popular. One is to include a unit totally devoted to review after every five or six units. Such a unit would have a study guide and study questions like any other unit. This offers an occasion for the instructor to provide and demand some

---

[1] Billy Koen, "Determining the unit structure in a PSI course." *Engineering Education*, March 1973, 432-434.

integrated overview of course material. An alternative is to include some review in all later units. The latter procedure might result in a sequence in which a review of Unit 1 is included in Unit 5, a review of Unit 2 is included in Unit 6, etc. This places a heavy burden on the proctors to be constantly familiar with every bit of information in the course. No doubt there are other satisfactory ways to handle the question, the point being that, unless integration and retention are of no concern, some systematic review should be planned in courses where the subject matter itself does not automatically produce it.

5. *Amount of material covered.* Most teachers find they must cover a little less in a PSI course. While it is commendable to always present as rich a content as possible, what is offered in the traditional course rarely equals what is learned. Although the traditional teacher may point with some pride to a very full syllabus, such a course content may prove unreasonable if the students must learn everything. Therefore, there is a need to examine the course content, make decisions about what is important and what is not, eliminate the superfluous, and with a slightly reduced syllabus take pride in the fact that the students will learn it.

Although there have been a few teachers who have reported they can cover more material in a PSI course, my impression is that approximately four-fifths of the normal course content is about the right amount to include in the corresponding PSI course. Once given successfully, there is a temptation to increase the total work load, increase the size or number of units, the next time the course is given. It is not surprising that the teacher watching his students master everything might feel he can teach more. Perhaps he can, but at some point he can add no more. There is a limit to the amount of work one can require for any given number of credits, as vaguely as that limit is defined. Students almost universally report that they work harder in PSI courses than in other courses. An appreciation of that fact and some concept of reasonableness and fairness should enter into the decision of whether or not to increase the scope, assignments, and requirements of the course the second time around.

6. *The study guide.* The study guide must allow the student to proceed through the textbook and other course materials largely on his own and do so successfully. This function is more important than whatever form the guide might take. Typically there are four standard sections.

a. *Introduction.* This section provides the opportunity for the instructor to comment on, supplement, or correct the textbook. There may be outdated sections of the text that require the addition

MANKATO STATE COLLEGE LIBRARY
MANKATO, MINNESOTA

of current information to be complete. An instructor may wish to change the stress or emphasis of some topics in the textbook to a view more compatible with his own. On other occasions the introduction might be directed toward a summary or synthesis of information the text fails to present, and/or toward the development of relations between units. Some of the things the teacher might have said in lecture can be included. It is a chance for the instructor to present his own opinions, interests, and style.

The introduction can be long or short. It can be formal or chatty. It should be interesting—interesting enough to lead students to read the assignment.

b. *Statement of objectives.* This section should specify the goals of the unit. The statement of objectives, in behavioral terms, tells the student what he should be able to do as a result of reading the unit. It allows the student to determine for himself when he has met the mastery criterion. It also requires the instructor to decide and indicate what is important in the assignment.

The more specific the statement of objectives the better. There exists a large amount of literature on writing behavioral objectives and it might be useful to consult a book on the subject.[2] The danger of this is that initially it may lead to writing almost by formula and the statement will appear mechanical and totally lacking in style. The trick is to be precise and interesting at the same time.

The list of objectives should direct the student to *all* of the information you intend to include on the unit tests. As noted elsewhere the tests should examine the student on each and every objective.

c. *Study questions.* In some disciplines the material is so discrete that general objectives are difficult to state. The information may not be combined easily into general goals. In such cases a list of study questions may replace the objectives statement. Even when unit objectives are given, study questions further help the student to detect his progress and success. This section may include a list of concepts or technical terms which the student should be prepared to define or other items where the problem is to provide an example.

Again, the study questions should be comprehensive, probing all information to be included on the unit tests. While the test questions and the study questions will not be exactly the same, they should refer to the same course content. Students may be asked to

---

[2] See for example, J. S. Vargas, *Writing Worthwhile Behavioral Objectives,* New York: Harper and Row, 1972.

write out their answers to the study questions. Proctors may occasionally ask to see these written answers, particularly when a student fails a unit test.

d. Procedure. The point of this section is to specify the activities which will prove adequate for the student to accomplish the unit objectives. In some cases this may be as simple as stating the assignment to be read and suggesting that the student answer the study questions before attempting a test. Perhaps a few added comments about what to skip, what to skim, and what to study in detail will be sufficient. Other units may require detailed instructions suggesting which pages should be read in which order, concurrently with which study questions, perhaps with a page-and-line key of special instructions where the book is inadequate or the material particularly difficult. A well-written procedure section tells the student what to do, how to self-test his comprehension, how to decide whether to proceed or review, and how to decide when he has finished. The procedure section is usually written as a series of suggestions rather than as a required prescription. The goal is never to leave the student wondering what to do next. He will probably decide to do something else.

In addition to the study questions, the study guide may include a self-test, written text supplements as additional parts of the assignment, or any other information, suggestions or hints that seem to help. The main criterion for a study guide is that it work.

7. Test format. Two aspects of the unit tests are dictated by pre-logistical considerations. First, mastery learning requires that the tests probe the students' understanding of each and every major unit objective rather than "sample" what has been learned. Second, the questions must relate to the objectives specified rather than tap some hidden agenda. Beyond that there is no standard format. In some PSI courses the test questions have been entirely essay, in others only objective items have been used. Physical science and engineering courses often require problem solutions. The system does not dictate test format, but there are some interlocking logistical considerations to influence the format eventually chosen.

It has already been noted that it is desirable to construct tests that can be answered in fifteen to twenty minutes. The nature of the material determines in part whether or not all of the unit objectives can be tested by a few essay questions or require a larger number of more objective items. It was also mentioned as desirable to construct tests which can be "corrected" in about five minutes to avoid putting too heavy a load on the proctors, creating waiting lines, or increasing the number of proctors required. Some kinds of questions can be graded more quickly than others. Finally, the tests must be such that the answers can be judged by the proctors. Obviously this favors objective questions, but not to the point of excluding essays. When more advanced students are used as proctors, more complex judgements can be left to their discretion without fear of decreasing quality control. Alternatively, regardless of the proctors' level of experience, the adequacy of the proctor materials (see below) determines how much discretion can be left to the proctors, while maintaining a uniform and precise high standard.

The pros and cons of all these considerations have resulted in a popular test format that is best described as "mixed." A typical example might be a ten question quiz, with two true-false questions, three multi-choice questions, two matching items, two complete-the-sentence questions and one short essay. Each instructor must consider his objectives, his discipline, the number and level of his proctors, the nature of his proctor material, and his own willingness to participate as final judge in determining his test format.

Whatever the decision, four alternative and equivalent forms of each test are generally required. I have mentioned elsewhere of having five, six, or more alternative forms. It now appears that any student who is unsuccessful after three attempts probably needs more careful guidance than a proctor can provide. It is now my practice to allow the proctor two attempts at remediation. After a third "failure" the student should see the professor for a more detailed analysis of his difficulties. This may call for some special instructions and the administration of the fourth quiz, or the on-the-spot construction of a special test by the teacher that aims directly at the sources of the problem. The repetitive administration of a general test over the entire unit now appears to be an undesirable shot-gun approach for those few students who cannot master a unit after three attempts. Here is another case where personalized attention is required, and in this instance, it is the teacher who should give it.

Many instructors writing test material find they have "run dry" after writing two test forms. A week later a third form seems to flow more easily. With three different forms in hand a fourth can usually be created by "stealing" questions from forms A, B, and C. When this is done, the selection of questions for the final form should not be random, but must be consistent with the concept that every test should probe every objective. Teachers with computer facilities available have found it useful to generate a large number of test forms from a fixed question pool. Again the permutations and combinations the machine can produce should be limited by the concept of complete rather than random testing.

8. Proctor materials In general, the job of the proctor is *not* to give away answers, but to decide on the adequacy of his students' answers and provide remedial instructions for those who have not met the high criterion of mastery. A "Proctor Answer Sheet," which is a listing of the correct answers, is helpful but in most cases inadequate. A list of page numbers or other informational instructions that the proctor can use to guide his students to correct their own mistakes is more useful. Ideally, the proctor materials will suggest supplementary questions that the proctor can ask. This will allow him to deal appropriately with the student who knows the answer but misreads the question, or those who do not know the material but appear to have attained mastery by a lucky guess. In this form the proctor's materials constitute a protocol for a structured interview.

Such complete proctor materials are highly recommended. They will call upon the proctor to quiz the student further on how he decided upon his answers, even where the answer is correct. It will allow for a reasonable and personalized solution when the problem is more in the ambiguity of the teacher's question than in the student's lack of understanding. The student-proctor interview virtually eliminates the possibility of cheating and adds to the personalized aspect of the course. When a proctor's function is merely to check off answers as "right" or "wrong," he could in fact be replaced by a machine. Then the course is no longer a PSI course and a great opportunity has been lost.

The problem, then, is to use the proctor in a way that fully utilizes the complex judgements only a human can make, without sacrificing precision, accuracy, and honesty. This will probably mean the proctor materials will indicate the types of errors which the proctor is not equipped to deal with and where the students should be sent directly to the teacher.

It is easier to write the proctor materials at the same time the tests are written than later on. With the passing of time, it becomes a task to find the page references useful to the proctors in guiding students who have made an error. Worse still, sometimes it becomes difficult to recall the point of the question or even remember the answer! The proctor materials develop quite naturally and easily when written concurrently with the tests.

The comprehensiveness and amount of detail needed in the proctor materials depends on (1) the level of training of the proctors relative to that of the students, (2) the type of test questions being used, and (3) the procedural decisions concerning the frequency of proctors' meetings. The need for a proctor manual which further defines the proctor's duties and even provides a brief course of training will depend upon the same three considerations.

II. Course Policy

Course policy decisions are normally announced in a course policy statement given to the student on the first day of class.

In a sense the course policy statement is additional course material. It explains to the student how the course will function. What to include in that statement and what course policy decisions must be made before it can be written are the subject of this section.

When PSI is new on campus, it may be useful to start out the course policy statement with a brief account of the features of PSI (mastery, self-pacing, etc.) and the benefits the student may expect from the method. In later semesters the word will have spread and this information is less necessary.

The policy statement will probably include all the information that might normally be given out in the form of a syllabus on the first day of any class: instructor's name, office number, office hours, course title, textbook(s), classroom number, etc. In the PSI course, there are several other matters to include:

1. *Grading policy*. This is of more than passing concern to the students and will need to be covered in detail. The ideal of PSI suggests a simple statement of the requirements for an *A* (passing all units, passing the final exam) with an alternative of an *Incomplete*.

In practice this is often difficult to establish within an existing college system which has rules and traditions surrounding the grading procedure. A popular compromise is to establish a grade equivalent for passing any given number of units such as all $18 = A$, $17 = A-$, $16 = B+$, $15 = B$, etc. While this does restore the normal grade categories, it has the advantage of specifying exactly what the various grades mean. Using the example above, a *C* means the student has mastered all the material through Unit 12 and knows nothing about the last six units. If there are later sequential courses at least it is clear what the C-student must do—he needs to go back and pass those last six units. Of course, there is nothing in the above example which implies the units and grades should be equated as given. Some instructors may find other combinations more suitable. (All 20 units $= A$, $19 = B$, $18 = C$ sounds like a rather harsh version.)

There is an alternative to the above procedure which is probably preferable, although more at variance with traditional practice. It is to retain only the A grade, the number of units completed determining how many credits of A have been earned. For example, in a twenty-unit course the student passing all twenty units would receive an A and the normal three credits associated with that course. The student successfully completing fifteen units would also receive an A but only two credits; the student finishing ten units might receive only one credit, but again with a grade of A. This system recognizes that the student has met a high standard and also indicates what proportion of the course has been mastered.

2. *Final exam policy.* Once some unit-grade scale is established, there are decisions to be made about a final examination. One question is whether or not to have one! There are those who feel it is inconsistent with the basic philosophy of PSI to give a final exam. If the student has mastered the course why is such an exam needed? There is much to be said for that argument. Nonetheless, it is probably wise to give a final.

The PSI teacher will have enough problems with his colleagues without attempting to break the final exam tradition as well. A final exam is useful to answer the inevitable challenge of whether or not all those A's represent a compromise with quality. Your exam can be compared with those given by others. Secondly, the final exam does provide a fine occasion for one last attempt to integrate all the bits and pieces of information. Further, since the final is consistent with the unit tests (the temptation to reveal at last your true but previously hidden agenda for the course would be downright dishonest), it presents no great threat to students who have, in fact, mastered the course. Finally, and to my mind the most compelling reason for a final exam is that it removes pressure from the proctors. Students who must do no more than pass all units to receive an A are not above using both bribery and profane charms on proctors who are susceptible. The proctor who can cast his prescription for remediation and a second test in terms of his desire to help the student prepare for his final judgment is in a much less vulnerable position. It is almost unfair to the proctor not to provide him with that graceful "out." The existence of a final provides the proctor with a legitimate reason for his decision that further study is needed.

Having decided to give a final exam we are left to decide its relative weight in determining the course grade. For no documented reason that I know of, many PSI teachers have adopted a procedure whereby the final equals twenty-five percent of the course grade, and the number of units completed (see above) comprises seventy-five percent. It does not seem like a bad solution. Other combinations would probably work as well, with the restriction that it would not fit the spirit of the course if the final exam determined the entire grade and all the unit tests counted for nothing!

In a well-run PSI course cheating is unlikely to occur. Students are working with individuals they come to know; they are not fighting a system. The temptation to beat a bureaucracy is not there, or it should not be. It also is difficult to cheat in a PSI course, although some will try. Their lack of mastery will show up on the final. For just such cases it is wise to include in the course policy statement the provision that the instructor reserves the right to count final exam scores that are in the *D* and *F* range more heavily. While this poses no threat at all to students who have done their own work, it does permit the instructor to reevaluate the course grades for those few students who have found some devious route to the last unit.

3. The early final. For those who pass all of the units before the end of the semester, one or two early final exams are generally offered. The option of being totally finished with the course before the normal exam period encourages many students to move ahead rapidly. In fact, to force these students to wait for the normally scheduled final might actually put them at a disadvantage.

One final given a month early and a second final given two weeks before the end of classes is generally sufficient—and three forms of the final exam are enough to write! The dates of these early exams can be specified only as it becomes possible to predict how many students will finish by any given time. Usually the final exam can only be taken once. To further encourage rapid progress, a few PSI courses have allowed those who finish early, take an early exam, and are not satisfied with the results of their first attempt to retake the final on the normally scheduled date. In practice this option does encourage students to finish early. However, the early finishers almost without exception score well on the final, and so the option to repeat the exam is rarely exercised.

4. Incomplete policy. This is a matter of great debate. The ideal of PSI is that students work until they finish the course, making semesters irrelevant. This should mean that students who have not finished all the units at semester's end are given an *Incomplete* and the opportunity to continue during the next semester. Where university rules make this liberal policy impossible the teacher must formulate some criterion for granting an *Incomplete* grade. Two rules often used are (1) some absolute minimum number of units passed—perhaps half of the total or (2) some characteristics of the student's record that shows sustained, if slow, progress.

Whatever rule is established it will probably cause problems. There have been PSI courses where *Incompletes*, other than for the usual health reasons, were not allowed. As liberal an *Incomplete* policy as possible is recommended. Of course the availability of the *Incomplete* should not be stated in a way that encourages procrastination. Some instructors feel it is best not to mention the *Incomplete* grade in the course policy statement. A rigid deadline sets a limit to the mastery requirement. Free access to the *Incomplete* may encourage delay. An *Incomplete* which must be earned (or justified) can protect the goal of mastery without producing procrastination.

5. *Unit test rules.* In some PSI courses students are limited to being tested on only one unit per day. Without such a limitation, a few students will prepare two, three, or more units at once and try to pass large segments of the course during the few classes they attend. This practice tends to defeat the reason that the course was divided into units in the first place. Other problems arise when students do more than one unit per day. Student error rate goes up and remediation becomes more difficult when several units are studied and tested simultaneously. The one unit per day limit works well. It can always be relaxed somewhat near the end of the semester for students who have proved able to deal with material and can probably handle larger assignments.

For students who do not pass a unit on the first attempt, second and third tests are available. It is common practice, however, to allow only two attempts on any one day. If a student is not successful on the second try, a pause with extensive review is probably necessary. In addition to a two-tests-per-day limit some instructors impose a thirty minute pause between the first and second tests, again to encourage restudy and review.

6. *Statement on the meaning of "pass."* The mastery requirement specifies that students are allowed to proceed from one unit to the next only after an essentially perfect performance. Many PSI instructors have chosen to interpret this as meaning nine out of ten questions answered correctly. Provided the proctor calls upon the student to correct even that one error (although not requiring another test) the "nine-out-of-ten" standard seems a satisfactory definition of mastery. Any further compromise with mastery is unwise. The requirement of eighty-five percent will automatically raise questions as to why eighty-three percent isn't "close enough." There will be requests for "partial credit." An adversary system with "bargaining" about grades quickly returns to the classroom. The mutual respect and high morale upon which the course depends deteriorates. The course policy statement should specify that the criterion for a pass is perfection. As difficult as it sometimes is to define mastery, it is less arbitrary than any number we can pick. The student-teacher discussion of why 79 is a *C* and 80 is a *B* is doomed to be

hostile, petty and indefensible before it even starts. The discussion of what we mean by mastery can take place on a higher level. The call for excellence should be loud and clear in the course policy statement.

7. Proctor assignment. Proctors typically are advanced undergraduates who have taken the course in a previous semester and been selected because of competence, interest, and personal qualities which are hopefully attractive or at least not abrasive. These students, called "external" proctors because they are no longer taking the course, must be compensated for their work. Money is an attractive reward but a successful course will probably spawn other courses, the number of proctors will increase, and the resulting strain on the department budget may become a serious limitation to further growth. Once established on campus as a paying job the tradition is hard to change. It is probably a bad choice. Course credit is a preferable reward. The proctors learn more than anyone so awarding course credit is certainly defensible. (Senior majors facing the GRE's could hardly find a better way to review than to proctor. They might even volunteer!) However compensated, external proctors are a stable group. This stability has many advantages and is a safe way to begin, if possible.

A fixed group of proctors can be specifically trained. The proctor materials (see above) can be less explicit because a weekly proctor meeting can be planned. These meetings provide valuable and lively occasions for the instructor to add to or modify written materials, for the proctors to provide feedback concerning recurrent problems or defects in the study guides or test questions, and for everyone to compare notes on how the course is going.

If external proctors are used the course policy statement should identify their qualifications — in a sense provide their status. With external proctors there is an additional decision to make. Given a fixed group of proctors it is possible to assign students to a specific proctor. The usual ratio is ten students per proctor. An assignment procedure has the obvious advantages of continuity and familiarity. Proctors develop a background of information about each of their students which is useful in pinpointing problems, suggesting remediation, and building a relation that reduces procrastination and adds to the morale and personalized character of the course. On the other hand, allowing students to consult with any proctor available, produces shorter waiting lines, avoids problems when a proctor is absent, and decreases the possibility of proctor bias.

The pros and cons of proctor assignment versus free-choice based on availability are probably sufficiently balanced that the decision becomes a matter of local conditions or even instructor style. The question is one of intimacy versus flexibility. Whatever the decision the course policy statement should give the student information concerning which proctor he should see.

8. *Internal proctors.* When money, course credit, and/or knowledge-able upperclassmen are not available the instructor may wish to initiate an "internal" proctor system. In this case the instructor evaluates the Unit 1 tests of the first few students. Those who pass become proctors for their colleagues on the material of Unit 1. The first students to be tested on Unit 2 are again evaluated by the instructor. These students replace the original group. The result is a group of proctors who are always in the lead. Quality control is assured since it is the instructor who serves as proctor for those students who are chosen to tutor their classmates. This process of using the first students to finish a unit as proctors is followed throughout the course.

Use of the internal proctor system results in a constantly changing group of proctors, which means that the proctor material must be more extensive, students can no longer be assigned to specific proctors, and proctor meetings will be more difficult to arrange and less useful. On the other hand, internal proctors require less review since they have just passed the units in question and no course credit or monetary compensation is required. Still internal proctors must be rewarded since, unlike their classmates, they are asked to come to class every testing day. This extra duty must be worthwhile. Awarding points to be counted towards a grade is the most obvious answer, but if grades are to be related to mastery they should not be used as rewards for other activities. While it is better to award a few points than to allow the course to flounder or fail, it is preferable to rely on other rewards.

There are some built-in benefits to proctoring. The most important benefit is the opportunity to learn more. Proctors invariably score well on the final exam. Proctors are quick to realize they do learn more and they pass this information on to their classmates. They are helpful in recruiting classmates to undertake the job. Some students will proctor for reasons they describe as "relating to self-confidence" and "prestige" and they appreciate the special attention they receive (see "special procedures" in Section III). Students about to apply for graduate school or a summer job find the proctor job a good way to get to know the professors. The instructor-proctor familiarity provides grist for a better letter of recommendation. The proctor position can be an "enrichment activity" for the above average student, a chance for recognition for students not normally singled out, and the best possible review procedure for all. There is the enticement of pay since one proctor will probably be chosen as next semester's course manager. The end-of-the-semester proctor party in itself probably convinces very few students to commit extra time, but the high morale such social occasions repre-

sent is more than sufficient reward in an increasingly large and deper-
sonalized system. There are many reasons why students will volunteer
to work as internal proctors and the more important ones relate to
mastery of the subject matter and personalized instruction.

If an internal proctor system is to be used, its operation should be
explained in the course policy statement. Since anyone proctoring
against his will would almost certainly make a bad job of it, the explanation of proctor selection should include the comment that the position
is voluntary for those students who qualify. A few students will be working rapidly to free their time for other commitments and they will not
want to have the proctor's responsibility of coming to class every day.[3]

9. *Class hours*. The scheduled class hours assigned for any regular
course are probably sufficient for a PSI course as well. With so much
material to be set out at the beginning of class and the filing and recording that must be done at the end, many PSI teachers prefer a Tuesday-
Thursday seventy-five-minute class to a Monday-Wednesday-Friday
fifty-minute schedule. Others prefer providing three opportunities per
week for students to take tests. It is not unusual for both the students
and the instructor to feel some need to extend the regular hours. While
a slight increase is a good and generous thing to do, if time and classroom space is available, it is not wise to double or triple the time available. The instructor has a function in the PSI classroom; he should be
there most of the time. If testing hours are extended the teacher tends to
become only an occasional visitor to his own course. Round-the-clock
testing may appear attractive, convenient, and flexible but it leads to
the phenomenon of the "lonely learner." If extended, the hours should
be sufficiently restricted so that the student will meet other students
and the instructor, when he arrives.

10. *Special announcements*. Some courses may require comment on
some of the following:

> a. *Lectures*. If lectures are to be scheduled perhaps a list of topics
> and dates can be included in the policy statement. If lectures or
> other events are available only to those who have passed a specific
> number of units or met other conditions, these regulations also
> need to be specified. A few lectures are useful. The instructor can
> serve as a model, impart style, even provide inspiration. In fact we
> might expect a very polished and challenging presentation now

---

[3]For a more complete discussion of the internal proctor system, see J. G.
Sherman, "A Permutation of an Innovation," in *Personalized System of Instruc-
tion: 41 Germinal Papers*, J. G. Sherman, ed., Menlo Park, Calif.: W. A.
Benjamin, Paper No. 29.

that such events are infrequent. Such lectures must be fine indeed; otherwise they will not attract an audience. Since the lecture is given for motivational reasons rather than for the transmittal of essential information, PSI lectures are "extras" and not required. They are usually poorly attended unless they are very, very good.

The scheduling of lectures is important. Lectures scheduled during normal class testing hours produce an audience of as few as one or two students; everyone is very busy getting on with the main task at hand. A few more students will appear if the testing session is cancelled. Unless the instructor wishes to give a lecture at a different time he must decide whether or not what he has to say is of sufficient importance to warrant calling a halt to the other activities of the course.

b. *Other Events.* The PSI course does not preclude field trips, audio-visual presentations, working at a computer terminal, or in fact any of the usual class related activities. The system has been designed to avoid hardware and instrumentation as essential features. However, if a campus already has such facilities, these can be put to very good use within the context of a PSI course, provided they do not produce a lock-step group pace in the course and there is some provision to insure that what the student does is followed by appropriate consequences. Participation in a discussion group is a possibility if for some reason it adds to the course. Since students working at different rates on different parts of the course have little in common when gathered together "at random," such discussions may have to be scheduled on a repetitive basis. Every time five students pass Unit 8 for example, they would form a group and get together for a discussion. This will mean there must be a series of discussion groups scheduled following Unit 8 to accommodate the pace of individual students. It can be done, but the scheduling problems are formidable. There must be a careful consideration of whether or not a discussion session, in fact, makes an important contribution to the course.

Certain subject matters at some levels do call for these special events and the course policy statement should describe their relation to other aspects of the course.

c. *Labs.* It is not necessary that all units be based on reading material. Our first PSI courses included laboratory units (see Chapters Two and Three). Lab session units were like any other units in that students went to the lab only when they had mastered the previous and prerequisite reading units. A lab assistant was there to assess the students' lab work and the criterion was mastery. While in some disciplines a self-paced lab may be difficult to implement because several experiments will have to be concurrently available over long periods of time, in others a self-paced lab can produce a cost saving by requiring less duplication of equipment than the normal lab.

d. Notice board. It is difficult for the teacher to make announcements since the class rarely meets as a whole. The course policy statement should specify a bulletin board where notices can be posted. Later grief can be avoided if it is clearly stated that students are responsible for checking the notice board at least once every ten days.

e. Postcards. Another aid in combatting the difficult communication problem is to ask each student to fill out two index cards with name, local address, and phone number on the first class day. These can easily be cut and attached to postcards that can be sent to "inquire about the health" of students who disappear for long periods of time.

f. Individual progress chart. Some instructors have found it useful to supply students with a graph on which they can plot their progress day by day or week by week. Sometimes these graphs have a line drawn in which indicates a suggested pace. Even more specific are charts that indicate a maximum and minimum rate; these rates describe the number of units which must be passed by any class day in order for the student to finish the course as rapidly as possible, and the number of units per class day which the student must pass in order to complete the last unit on the last testing day of the semester. Some instructors report that the inclusion of such a graph in the course policy statement combats procrastination by making visible to the student the pace at which he is working.

g. A special warning. The student in a PSI course has great control over his own activities. It is probably wise to advise him that this responsibility has a danger. You may wish to invite those who have not developed good study habits and the needed self-control to consult with you as to how to manage the freedom the system provides. A few students may wish to set up a contract system until they learn how to manage their own behavior. No student plans to fail; a few students fail to plan and need a little help to learn the skills of self-control.

h. Keep the rules simple. While all of the above comments on course policy may seem complicated, there have been courses constructed with twice as many rules and regulations. Some teachers working with "token" systems have designed courses where points are available for almost everything, all on a sliding scale that changes with the day of the week, the number of tests taken, etc. Some complexities may be appropriate for those who are teaching PSI courses with a research interest in contingency management or behavior modification. Otherwise we recommend that the course policy be kept as simple as possible. The goal is a course that the instructor can live with. Simple systems are more durable.

III. Implementation and Daily Procedure

It is with respect to this aspect of logistics that there are the fewest rules but perhaps the greatest number of decisions to be made. Again, *making* a decision, in most cases, is more important than which of the alternatives is chosen.

1. Physical facilities. There are very few special requirements for physical facilities. If studying, testing, and proctoring are all occurring in the same room, then that room should be large. There is a lot of movement and a lot of talking in a PSI course. Cramped quarters, blocked isles, and the constant buzz of other conversations in the background can make the whole atmosphere unpleasant. Adequate space, flexible seating that can be moved to accommodate traffic flow, good lighting, and a carpet on the floor to decrease noise make an ideal setting. In such a large room, those taking tests are generally asked to sit in front, those studying sit toward the back, and student-proctor stations, well separated from each other, can be set up along both sides. If such accommodations are not available, it is best to use two rooms; one for studying and test taking, the other for the student-proctor interviews. Some PSI classrooms have been set up with special booths or cubicles for proctoring. The privacy decreases distractions, but makes it more difficult for the instructor to monitor what is going on and to appear casual when he decides to sit in on an interview. The only essential "instruments" consist of a long table or other suitable working surface on which to spread out materials and records in the front of the room and a file cabinet, which can be locked and left in the testing room.

2. Study guides and other materials. In a small course someone might be delegated to hand out the next study guide to students whenever they pass a unit. Originally, we thought that the receipt of a new assignment might serve as a reward for a job well done. Tight control was maintained over the study guides; students received new assignments only when they qualified by passing a test on the previous unit. Irrespective of whether or not this is a naive view of reward, in a large class this does not work. Study guides are quickly available in the dormitories and the fraternity houses, so there seems little point to attempt to police their availability. When freely available, spread out on the front table in the classroom, students are more likely to take them only when needed than when a check-out system is involved. In any case, after two or three revisions you will probably want to have the study guides printed and sold in the college bookstore, if only to save on the duplication costs charged against the department budget. In the meantime, someone must be assigned the job of making Xerox copies, collating, and setting out these materials.

3. *The tests.* Because of the personalized nature of the proctor interview, most PSI teachers report that cheating is not a common problem. Even more reassuring, students who have graduated continue to maintain that cheating is less frequent on PSI tests than on the examinations associated with more traditionally taught courses. In any case, some procedure is necessary, particularly for large classes, to prevent tests from being stolen.

One procedure is to have a limited and known number of copies of each test form. Each copy is numbered. When ready for a test, the student goes to the course manager at the front desk and "signs out" a test for Unit x, Form y, Copy z. Typically, a course might have eighteen units, four test forms for each unit, with ten copies of each form numbered and available. The record might show that a student had in his possession Copy 7, of Form C, on Unit 12. When finished with a test, the student returns it to the course manager, has his name checked off, and is then no longer responsible for that test form. On any given unit, the alternate test forms are normally given out in "random" order. That is, students do not necessarily receive Form A for their first attempt, Form B for their second try, etc. Students then cannot predict which form they will receive on any given occasion.

4. *The answer sheet.* If the above test form procedure is followed, students are asked not to write answers on the test form itself (these are used again), but on a special standardized answer sheet. These answer sheets should have spaces indicating (1) unit, (2) form, (3) student's name, (4) date, (5) proctor's name, and (6) a place to indicate pass or fail. It is the answer sheet the student takes to his proctor for the process of interview, comment and correction. In smaller courses, students may be asked to write their answers in a continuing blue book. This gives the teacher a chance to spot check the work and write a note to the student, and indirectly, to the proctor.

5. *Record keeping.* There are many ways to handle the large amount of paper that the system requires. One solution is to keep a manila folder for each student. At the end of the class period each proctor files the answer sheets or blue books he has corrected in the appropriate student folders, and enters the date, unit, form, "grade," and his own name on the cover of the folder. Thus collected, the student's total history of successes and problems are quickly available for inspection when the instructor is called upon to prescribe a solution to any particular difficulty. It is possible by reviewing past tests to spot the kind of question, or some pattern of errors that is a recurrent source of difficulty. By a quick check of the folder cover, it is possible to get a rapid reading concerning the student's pace, error rate, any possible proctor bias, and to intercept students who take the same form of a unit test twice or decide not to take the course sequentially.

6. *Proctor folders.* The proctors will need copies of every test form for every unit as well as the expanded answer sheets and any special instructions. With a fixed group of external proctors, these proctor materials can be assembled in advance. If internal proctors are used, the materials should not contain information on units the proctor himself has not passed, and the course manager must then add new materials to the proctor folders as appropriate. With internal and therefore a changing group of proctors, there should be a space on the cover of the proctor's folder for recording who has proctored, through which unit, how many times, and on which dates.

7. *The course manager.* In small courses, the instructor can oversee many of these daily procedural details or ask the proctors to take turns at the job. In larger courses one person, the course manager, is needed to deal with materials and record keeping. He is usually paid similarly to normal course assistants or T.A.'s.

The course manager is responsible for much of what has been said concerning implementation. He has a few other duties. He should: (1) see to it that study guides, answer sheets and other materials are duplicated, collated and available, and that the test forms are numbered; (2) arrive in the classroom early to rearrange seating if necessary, open the file and set out materials; (3) pass out tests and monitor the test check-out system (the sign-up sheet) during the class; (4) consult the student record files when students cannot remember which test forms they have already taken on any given unit; (5) supervise the answer sheet filing and the recording of student progress after class; (6) check that all test forms are accounted for at the end of each test session; (7) insure that the folders containing proctor materials are kept up-to-date and that these are returned and secured after each class day; (8) answer routine questions concerning course policy; (9) pinch hit as a proctor in a crisis and answer course content questions (if equipped to do so).

From the job description, it is clear that the course manager's duties are mostly clerical. There is not much education in it for the manager, except when he pinch hits as a proctor. The manager should probably be paid rather than given course credit and be made aware beforehand that his job is important but not particularly stimulating. That is why he is paid! If a graduate student is given this job perhaps he can collect additional data for research purposes, which will also serve to add some interest to the routine duties.

8. The proctor. His role is described in the course policy statement and in the proctor's materials. He arrives before class, obtains his proctor folder from the course manager, and conducts student interviews, passes his students on to the next unit, or suggests which sections of the assignment need further study, or refers students to the instructor. He retains student answer sheets during the class session, files them in the student folders before leaving for the day, and brings the folder cover information up to date.

9. The student. His role is well described in the course policy statement and in the study guides. He comes into the classroom at times of his own choice, studies in the back of the room, receives tests, answer sheets, and signs out test forms with the course assistant in the front of the room, takes tests sitting in the first few rows, proceeds to his proctor when finished, leaves his answer sheet with the proctor, returns the test form to the course manager, and then picks up a new unit assignment, restudies preparing for an alternate form, or confers with the instructor depending on the outcome of his quiz performance.

10. The instructor. Aside from occasional lectures, the instructor's classroom duties are to monitor all aspects of the system, arbitrate disputes, provide special remediation for those who do not pass a unit after three attempts, and be available for consultation on any matter the course manager and proctors cannot handle. Some students will ask questions the proctors cannot answer, others will require exceptions from course policy rules no one else has the authority to give. Because the instructor's job is no longer routine, it is hard to predict. He is using his talents to provide answers to unique problems. He has a creative role in a PSI course. Of course, outside of class he must choose a text, prepare and revise the study guides, tests, and proctor materials, hold proctor meetings, and confer with the course manager. Most instructors report that teaching a PSI course is more work, but also more rewarding than teaching a more traditional course.

11. *Special procedures.*

a. Some instructors maintain a class progress wall chart on which is entered a record, by date, of each unit passed for each student. Opinion on this practice is divided; some teachers feel it is a motivating device, others view this as punitive and embarrassing for those who are proceeding slowly.

b. In courses with internal proctors, things run more smoothly if the first few minutes (perhaps ten) of each session are reserved for just proctors or potential proctors to take unit tests. This gives the instructor some uninterrupted time to correct the work of his proctors, thereby insuring that they are qualified. It also means that the proctors have finished their own work and are in position to help their colleagues by the time testing is open to the class in general.

Getting Started

There are a few suggestions that can be made to the person planning a PSI course for the first time.

1. *Pre-logistics.* It is tempting to challenge from the outset one or more of the essential features of PSI. The doubt may even be well taken, but it is a poor way to start. Research, which is increasingly taking the direction of a component analysis of the system, is now experimenting with deviations from the original format. From such research we can hope for a clarification of why PSI works and perhaps gain some ranking of the importance of the essential characteristics. This information will form a data base for making logistical decisions and should eventually lead to the designing of a better system. But initially, those new to PSI might do well to accept the defining characteristics as given and take a conservative position with respect to logistical decisions. Some "small" changes have led to major difficulties. The basic format works. There is no need to claim it to be the ultimate answer in order to give the advice that it is a proven safe way to start and makes a good baseline for judgement for those who wish to tinker with the system on the second try. The first time, however, follow the book!

2. *Choosing which course to program.* Often the instructor does not have this choice, but if he does, there are some things to consider. It is

better to try your hand for the first time with a course you know well and have taught before. It is also helpful if there is a good textbook, one with which you are already familiar. If others have already prepared PSI materials for that text, their model can cut down on the work you have to do, even if you choose to write your own version of the study guides.

Given a choice between an introductory fact-oriented course and a more advanced abstract one, it is easier to start out writing study guides for topics where the objectives are easily stated and generally agreed upon. The challenge of the more creative course leaves you with something exciting to do next year.

Because of the investment of time and effort involved in preparing a PSI course, it is wise to choose a relatively stable subject that might be expected to remain current for several years. The rapidly changing developments in the field of bio-genetics, or a course in current events makes these poor choices to begin with unless you are willing to engage in major revisions every year. The same considerations suggest that courses which will eventually serve fifty or a hundred students are more logical candidates from the point of view of cost effectiveness than courses with smaller enrollments.

3. *A small mistake is generally easier to correct (or hide) than a big one.* Start small. A class of twenty-five, perhaps an "honors section," is a good beginning. Even with careful planning, something will go wrong. It is easier to inform and less embarrassing to admit of a mistake to twenty-five people than to a hundred and fifty. The benefits that come with teaching large numbers of students can be claimed in the second year with considerably less danger. It is even desirable to have a re-duced teaching load the first time, if at all possible. The better students from this group will make fine, experienced proctors next year in your first large PSI course. In the meantime, with twenty-five students, you and one assistant can, if necessary, do all the proctoring while you get a feel for what that job entails. Even if you have proctors for this first course (internal or external), the instructor probably should serve as proctor at least part of the time to become familiar with the skills in-volved.

4. *Get as far ahead with writing your materials as possible.* There are many other things to do once the course starts. It is a terrible thing to be only one unit ahead of the class leader. The constant pressure to write a new unit each day can lead you to hate your best student! It is probably unwise to start a PSI course unless at least half the units are written before the first class meeting. It is even better to have the whole course ready. There is always one person who moves ahead faster than you

would predict. Devoting a full summer to the preparation of materials for a one semester course is about right.

5. *Don't publish these materials quite yet.* No matter how carefully written, your materials will probably not be student-proof. What appears to be the most clear and lucid of prose in the quiet of the teacher's study will take on new shades of meaning in the classroom. In trying to get on with the job of writing materials, it is best to recognize they will not be perfect, so do the best you can, but don't worry about perfection for the first version.

Considering their untested state, all materials should be reproduced in a flexible, cheap, and easily modifiable form. A ditto machine is useful at this stage. If you make it easy on yourself to make corrections, you will be more likely to act on the feedback you get, change your study guides, your tests and the proctor materials, and produce a better course next year. After the second course, and the second round of corrections, it may be time to talk to a publisher.

6. *If in doubt, have too much of everything.* Too many proctors are better than too few. The same is true for the number of units in the course, the number of test forms per unit, and the number of instructions and objectives in the study guide.

7. *Keep a record of everything.* PSI makes learning visible. By leaving a record, the system is potentially self-corrective. Make use of this opportunity.

8. *Keep the rules simple.*

9. *Stay in your classroom and talk to everyone.*

Anyone who has followed this chapter in designing his course is not likely to fail. *These* materials are not perfect so the degree of that success is uncertain. It therefore seems appropriate to wish you good luck!

CHAPTER FIVE

PSI and Reinforcement Theor

Fred S. Keller

Since the first third of the present century, there has been a major change in our views concerning learning and the conditions of its occurrence. This change has been embedded within a system of behavior known by some as *reinforcement theory*—a system that arose from *the experimental analysis of behavior,* both animal and human. The architect of this change was B.F. Skinner, a psychologist who is today regarded as one of the twentieth century's leading figures. His researches, more than those of any other, may be said to have shown the way to effective education in our times. Anyone who uses PSI and wants to know its rationale, or anyone who would improve upon the format, would be well advised to study reinforcement theory and its application to the teaching problem.[1]

---

[1]A brief introduction, and a good one, to reinforcement theory is J. A. Dinsmoor's *Operant Conditioning: An Experimental Analysis of Behavior.* Dubuque, Iowa: Wm. C. Brown Co., 1970. A similar account, written expressly for the layman, is F. S. Keller's *Learning: Reinforcement Theory.* Rev. ed., New York: Random House, 1969. For the reader who cares to go further, two books by Skinner are especially recommended: *Science and Human Behavior.* New York: Macmillan, 1953; and *The Technology of Teaching.* New York: Appleton-Century-Crofts, 1968.

Some Principles of Behavior

Justice cannot be done to reinforcement theory in this chapter or this book. Mention can be made, however, of the more important principles of the system, to let the reader glimpse the kind of thinking that led to PSI and on which we think its future will depend.

1. Behavior is learned (conditioned, strengthened) through *reinforcement,* the rough equivalent of *reward.* Reinforcement occurs when certain events are *brought about* by the behavior or when others are *eliminated,* or reduced in their degree. A laboratory subject, for example, may be reinforced for some response because it gets him food or drink, or because it rids him of intense heat, light, or electric shock. The response in question is *strengthened* because its probability of recurrence, in a similar situation, has been heightened. In the laboratory, strength is commonly measured in terms of frequency of response.

2. Already-learned, already conditioned behavior can be weakened (decreased in probability of recurrence) by discontinuing reinforcement. *Extinction,* a word we got from Pavlov, is the term for this. If an organism's behavior will no longer produce the food or eliminate the shock, its rate of responding will drop in time to the pre-conditioned level, with the probable accompaniment of *anger* or *frustration.*

3. *Punishment* of behavior can decrease its frequency of recurrence. When the consequence of some response is a strong electric shock, a blast of sound, or other intense stimulation, there will be a decrease in the strength of the response—its frequency may decline or it may stop entirely. *Fear* may be evoked and any behavior of escape from the situation will be reinforced.

4. When behavior is strengthened (reinforced, conditioned) in one stimulus situation and weakened (extinguished) in certain others, a *discrimination* may be formed and the *stimulus control* of the behavior is achieved. An animal may come to respond in light but not in darkness; a child may come to "tell the difference" between a robin and a crow.

5. Those stimuli in the presence of which behavior has been reinforced or punished will themselves become rewarding or aversive. They are then called *secondary* or *conditioned reinforcers* or, in the second case, *conditioned aversive stimulation.* The bell that leads us to the dinner table becomes rewarding in itself, just as the sound of the dentist's drill becomes aversive.

6. A special class of secondary reinforcers, at the human level, are the *generalized reinforcers*, so-called because they strengthen behavior regardless of any special deprivation (for example, of water or of food) that prevails within a person at the time of their appearance. These include the *attention*, the *approval*, the *affection*, and the *submissive behavior* shown to us by other persons. In addition to these, there are the *token rewards*, including such things as money, diplomas, medals, or even academic A's.

7. Responses may be altered in one or more of their aspects even when the stimulus environment remains unchanged in any obvious way. A student may learn to pronounce a foreign word correctly or a basketball player may improve his shots as a result of reinforcement, but in the absence of changes in the external stimulus situation. The selective reinforcement of successive small approximations to some desired form of behavior is technically known as the *differentiation of response*, but the common term is *shaping*.

Shaping is often used to denote more complex matters than those described above — matters involving changes in *stimulus control* as well as changes in response. Thus, one is said to shape a hospital patient's behavior by little steps to engage in greater social interaction with other persons. Shaping is also said to occur in programmed-textbook learning. In both of these examples, however, the change that comes about is more often a shift in stimulus control than it is a change in the form of the response involved.

The seven principles cited here do not exhaust the armament of behavior science, but they are especially important in connection with the "psychology" of PSI. The designers of the system had the goal of maximizing the rewards for educational behavior, minimizing chances for extinction and frustration, eliminating punishment and fear, and facilitating the development of precise discriminations. They tried to use as many forms of generalized reinforcement as they could within the classroom, and they followed the rule of "successive small approximations" in the shifting of control from one stimulus situation to another or in the shaping of response itself.

From the point of view of reinforcement theory, the task of changing behavior, including that which we desire in the field of education, is one of making appropriate reinforcements dependent upon specific instances of human conduct in clearly denoted environmental circumstances. From this it follows that any "learning situation" in which the task is not identified or is unclear, in which the critical behavior is or can be absent, and in which the rewards are not assured, is not a learning situation in the proper meaning of the term.

This eliminates from serious consideration as a teaching method the usual lecture, the usual classroom demonstration, the usual discussion group, and the usual assignment of a paper to be written. In none of these is the behavior guaranteed or optimal reinforcement provided, even when the tasks are well defined. Learning *may* occur in all these situations; therapy may occur in some (for example, in discussion); but each one is deficient in one or more of the requirements for effective teaching.

This three-term rule should be invoked whenever any change in PSI is suggested to the user of our plan. Will the basic stimulus situations (the study material, the instructions, the objectives, the sample problems, the study questions) for each individual student be adequately presented to him? Are the appropriate responses guaranteed? And is there prompt and frequent reinforcement for such responses in such situations?

Educational Behavior

More than one kind of behavior is included in the educational process. First of all, perhaps, is that involved in *study of the printed page*—those rapid, ever-shifting patterns of response to stimulation from the textual material and from those intra-verbal chains, those "associations of ideas," which this material sets up within the reader. Such *study behavior* can be found in any teaching system, but it is especially encouraged under PSI, as will be seen below.

A second class of student behavior in the teaching-learning process may be called *supportive*. In order to receive assignments and be tested on the outcome of his study, a student has to go to school! Once there he has to carry out instructions, move from place to place at designated times, and go through various routine acts. He must do this almost daily, for weeks and months on end, in connection with every course of study he pursues.

Collateral behaviors must be carried out as well. He must engage in laboratory exercises, go on field trips, solve the library system, and take part in other academic or semi-academic matters related to his work. (If to these we were to add behaviors that the educational institution may encourage although they have no scholarly or professional aim, it can be seen that only a small percentage of a student's time is spent in actual textbook study.)

The success of any teaching system will be apparent in the strength of such supportive and collateral behavior. Their *weakness* will be shown in absences, in dropouts, and in low achievement records. It will appear in negative reactions toward the school and to its teachers. It may sometimes be reflected in acts of open rebellion or destruction. On the other hand, the *strength* of such behaviors will be seen in high records of attendance, in excellence of achievement, in a lowered drop-out rate, in positive attitudes toward the subject matter taught, as well as in loyalty to the institution.

PSI is scarcely ten years old and has not been used exclusively in many settings. But the data that we have today tells us that this method of instruction is at least as effective in the strengthening of study, sup-portive, and collateral behaviors as are the more traditional systems that we know. But PSI provides for still another kind of behavior, one that may be more important in the long run than any of those already men-tioned. The interaction of a student with his proctor not only makes for better academic understanding, but for emotional conditioning as well. The student comes to *like* the proctor and the proctor to like the stu-dent, and this conditioning is based primarily on what the other *knows*, rather than what he looks like, what he owns, how popular he is, or how he may perform in other fields. This is the kind of human interstimula-tion and response that makes a teaching method something more than a device for inculcating knowledge or imparting skills, however important these may be.

Available Reinforcers

What are the reinforcers in our plan? Which ones apply to the student and which ones to the proctor? What keeps the instructor happy at his work, or the assistant? Some answers to these questions have been sug-gested in other chapters of this book, but let us now consider them within the context of our theory.

For the *student* working under PSI, there are many payoffs. Some of these are not peculiar to the system, some vary in importance with the individual, and some are poorly understood. Among the latter are the subtle reinforcers that come with study of a text—those little explosions of satisfaction or relief from tension that come with understanding, as when the answer to a question may be found, when a new relationship of fact or theory is uncovered, or when some fresh application of a prin-ciple suggests itself to the reader. Such rewards would seldom be suffi-cient alone to keep study behavior strong, at least for the average stu-dent in a modern school. Textbooks usually lack the built-in reinforce-ments found in a work of fiction.

Getting ahead, unit by unit, within the system, provides a more important kind of payoff. In PSI, each step along the road produces a fraction of the student's final A. This is a *token reward* for many students, although perhaps not all. For most of them it will directly strengthen their engagement in the testing-grading process, and indirectly help them with their study. With each successive *A*, the final *A* comes closer, and the stronger the student's motivation seems to be. One is tempted to assert that, in this kind of system, the sum of all the *partial* grades is greater than the *whole* in its effect.

Other aspects of the system serve a similar function. *Small work units*, for example, lead to greater density of reinforcement than do large ones, such as those which typify the lecture system. Together with *self-pacing*, they also help the student to use those times for study in which counter-attractions do not compete for his behavior.[2] *Study questions* and *sample problems*, arranged in the order of treatment in the text, help the student focus on the relevant features of his task, thereby reducing the chances of extinction and increasing the frequency of success.

Immediate grading of unit tests encourages the reinstatement of responses made to questions and to strengthen further those that were correct. Also, the opportunity to clarify an answer and, if necessary, to defend it, may sharpen a student's discriminations and lead to a refinement of his concepts. Finally, the chance to take another test, with no penalty for failure, not only increases the probability of success, but also decreases fear of the testing situation.

The *proctor* is the greatest agent of reward. He is the source of several generalized reinforcers—*attention, approval,* and even *affection,* as well as the *token reward* of A that he hands out with the passing of every unit test. He never punishes the student for anything he does, and he often cues him (provides the discriminative stimulus) to behave in a manner that will guarantee some academic gain. He may help extinguish the anxiety or fear which the testing-grading situation arouses in the student. Finally, the proctor is the one who provides the early feedback from the student's test performance and permits him to defend his answers. No wonder students say, "the proctors are the greatest!"

There are generalized reinforcers for the *proctor* as well as the students. In every grading session, for example, he receives the close attention of his students to everything he says or does. His approval is courted, his advice is often followed and, with rare exceptions, there is submission to his judgment in the grading operation. He is treated with

---

[2] Frequent tests, when *teacher-paced*, are probably more aversive to the college student than are the standard midterm and final examinations—studying for them is almost certain to collide with more rewarding matters.

respect, which can be seen in the nod of agreement, the word of thanks, and the responsive smile. His opinion may even be sought on other than academic matters.

The proctor is also reinforced by the signs of progress in his wards, which he takes to be a measure of his own success. He draws special satisfaction from the improvement of those students whose performance at the beginning of the course was very poor. His gratification when a student correctly answers a difficult question, solves a knotty problem, or passes a readiness test without an error is often clearly apparent, and the reinforcement which he then delivers to the student is obviously "from the heart."

Proctors also commonly receive the token reward of money, or two points of academic credit (plus or minus one) for their work. The former usually has less appeal than does the latter, but neither may be essential in order to keep them on the job. Such reinforcers are too remote from daily function to have direct effect upon it, but they are appreciated at the course's end and may add to the attractiveness of the proctor's task for others, serving as incentives for seeking or accepting the position.

Other possible sources of reinforcement for the proctor would include the esteem of those above him in the system—the assistant and the instructor; the general enhancement of his status with his family, his peers, and with teachers of other courses; and especially, the increase in his knowledge of the course's subject matter—the improvement in his readiness to deal effectively with the concepts and to show his mastery of related skills. These reinforcers may not be easily identified in an objective way, and they are obviously interconnected, but they are almost always mentioned by those who hold a proctor's position for any length of time.

The reinforcements for the graduate (classroom) assistant are the hardest to describe because his work within the system is so varied. He may function as a proctor on occasion, serving in the study hall, in testing, or in grading. At other times he may replace the teacher, presiding over proctors' meetings, preparing demonstrations, and checking the performance of students and proctors. The reinforcement he receives from these and related duties is substantial, but probably does not add up to that of either the instructor or the proctor. The proctor, for example, has the benefit of his own increased knowledge and the continuous improvement of his special group of students; and the instructor has rewards that come from his successful operation of the system as a whole.

In addition, the assistant is likely to be burdened with housekeeping chores that do not augment his academic stature. Partly because of historical reasons, and partly because of the novel features of the system, his role may not be as rewarding as it should be. Perhaps, in any course where he is really needed, his early autonomy in the teaching function should be encouraged.

The *instructor's* reinforcements under PSI derive from several sources. Some of them come from a better appreciation of his course's content and a more intimate knowledge of his pupils' problems with it. Others come from the enthusiasm of his proctors, their growth in understanding, and their heightened comprehension of the teacher's task. Still others come from the increased consideration and respect he gets from everyone, whether student, proctor, or assistant. For the dedicated teacher there is satisfaction in the academic progress of each student and in the related growth in self-respect that he exhibits.

Aversive Features of the Plan

There is another side to the coin of reinforcement in our system, one that is difficult to avoid. When a student passes a unit test, for example, his next assignment comes as a reward, but it also constitutes a *threat* which can only be removed when the next test has been taken. The study questions, prepared for each assignment to show the student his objectives, also served this function. Each one is an obstacle to be surmounted before it is possible to go ahead. And behind these threats lie bigger ones—for example, the threat of lost approval, lost time, or lost assurance of the final A.

These aversive situations decrease in their importance for the student as the course goes on. The behavior of studying and taking tests, like that of swimming or bicycle riding, may be initially strengthened through avoidance. The swimmer avoids submersion and the cyclist avoids a fall. The student's reinforcement for answering study questions or taking a unit test may at first be an escape from the threat or painful consequences. Later on, with continued progress and no punishing events, the relevant stimuli become *rewarding* (secondary reinforcers) and the student actually enjoys the tests which he hated so much before. He likes to display his understanding and his skill.

The work of the proctor may also have aversive features. If he is over-generous or over-severe in grading, it will soon be brought to his attention; if a student seems to fail too often or is absent from the course too long, it will cause him a certain amount of worry. If another proctor's students are more advanced than his, this will also make him anxious. And so on. But the positive aspects of the course outweigh the negative, and most of his cares will vanish as his proficiency increases.

The instructor, too, is not without his doubts and fears, especially in his first term with the plan. He frets about the capacity of his pupils and their willingness to do the work required. He fears that the proctors will not be effective and that their interest will not continue. He is over-sensitive to the adverse comments of his colleagues and he is doubtful of administrative backing. He is frequently annoyed by his badly written questions, as well as his study units that are too easy or too hard. He may feel, not without good reason, that the time he spends in the improvement of his teaching will not be as effective as research in leading to promotion or to a raise in pay. He will vividly recall the colleague who was voted "most effective teacher," but whose "production" failed to get him tenure. As in the case of students and proctors, however, most of his anxieties will disappear as time goes on.

Footnote

The technology of teaching is a many sided matter. A pared-down statement of some principles of behavior, a classification of responses to various educational situations, and an enumeration of available reinforcers will not in themselves suffice for teaching *via* PSI. Practical considerations, such as those described in Chapters Three and Four, will have their place, together with a knowledge of the subject-matter field and a strong desire to teach. However, to improve upon this system or to devise a better plan, an understanding of behavior theory is important. If it isn't *reinforcement theory*, it will have to be some other.

CHAPTER SIX

PSI Today

J. Gilmour Sherman

PSI over the last five years can be generally characterized by the increasing diversity of disciplines involved, the varying character of institutions experimenting with the method, the accumulating research and literature, the initiation of conferences and workshops, the establishment of funded centers for research and dissemination, and the publication of a newsletter. Interest and growth in the method has been so rapid that "PSI Today" quickly comes to mean "PSI Yesterday."

PSI first began to excite interest during 1965-67 when it was being tried out at Arizona State University. It was discussed at conferences such as those of the American Psychological Association, the American Education Research Association, etc. Perhaps more influential than any of these discussions was the publication of "Goodbye, Teacher..." by F. S. Keller in 1968.[1] This article was read by many people, not all of them psychologists. Ben A. Green, Jr., a physicist at M.I.T. and Billy V. Koen, a nuclear engineer at the University of Texas at Austin, started PSI

---

[1]In *Journal of Applied Behavior Analysis*, 1, 1968, 79-80. Also in *Personalized System of Instruction: 41 Germinal Papers*, J. Gilmour Sherman, ed., Menlo Park, Calif.: W. A. Benjamin, 1974, Paper No. 1.

courses and published their experiences. Reflecting, in large measure, the lead of these two, the majority of today's PSI courses which are not in psychology are offered in the disciplines of physics and engineering.

But PSI is attracting those from other disciplines as well. A workshop in PSI methods, supported by the National Science Foundation, held in August 1971 at M.I.T. was attended by twenty teachers of math, chemistry, biology, and sociology as well as physics. The workshop was a two-week how-to-do-it affair which has become the model for others in the United States and Latin America. The basic format that was developed has been used ever since: after two or three days of introduction to the major features of the system, each instructor spends most of his time preparing material for the PSI course he intends to teach, with advice and suggestions from a staff member who has had experience teaching such courses. Several hundred teachers have now attended such workshops. Some teachers have been successful in their attempts to start PSI courses without such formal preparation, merely by reading the accumulating literature—but there have also been some failures, and reports of confusion and stress for the instructor who starts out alone. The two-week workshop, however, has produced a high proportion of successful courses and seems worth the investment. In less developed countries where there is a severe shortage of trained teachers and large segments of the population expecting and demanding access to education for the first time, the investment in a PSI workshop is less than the cost and time of alternative teacher-training programs.

Growing research data and interest precipitated the October, 1971 "Keller Plan" conference at M.I.T., attended by over 350 teachers and administrators. The conference was notable not only for the diversity of disciplines represented but also for the heterogeneous character of the institutions involved. Perhaps a third of the participants came from junior and community colleges, vocational schools, secondary schools, and educational institutions other than four-year colleges and universities. The papers reported at this conference made it clear that PSI was not a method suited only for superior students in "Ivy League" colleges or large state universities. Formal and informal accounts noted that self-pacing offered advantages, albeit different ones, to both the well-prepared or "bright" scholar and to the ill-prepared or less able student. The proctor function was described as a new kind of challenge for rapid learners who were often bored by the lack of stimulation in traditional courses geared to the average student. Other PSI teachers commented that being appointed a proctor had miraculous effect on the attitude and self-respect of the slower learners who eventually do qualify—students who had never before received recognition for mastery and competence in the traditional classroom. The unit perfection requirement appealed to all in its recognition of mastery as an appropriate goal of education.

This conference was followed by others—at Rice University in March, 1972, at Long Beach, California in November 1972, and in Washington, D.C. in April, 1974. Each conference grew in both size and diversity. These conferences did not test the limits of the system. These limits have yet to be tested (see Chapter Eight). The conferences did, however, change all previous estimates and guesses concerning inherent limitations of the method imposed by subject matter, student quality, educational level, and institutional character.

The conferences also provided a first forum for research reports, many of which have been presented at subsequent meetings of various professional societies and published as journal articles. In the last five years the literature has grown beyond what could reasonably be surveyed here, but other sources are available. John Hess has compiled "A Bibliography of Operant Instructional Technology in Higher Education" and a "PSI Psychology Course Catalog."[2] Both include information on a wide range of recent innovations as well as a comprehensive listing of PSI articles. A bibliography, "Individualized Instruction in Higher Education," prepared by Robert S. Ruskin, lists all known papers about PSI as of December, 1973.[3] Information and data are also available in edited papers, four collections of which have been published to date.[4]

The papers, articles and research reports on PSI now number over three hundred. The consistency of the reported results makes summarizing a simple matter. Most research reports have taken the form of comparing a PSI course with a "corresponding" traditional lecture course. Two comparisons are usually made, one between measures of achievement, such as final exam scores, the other between measures of preference and attitude using ratings on a questionnaire.

---

[2]Both are available from the PSI Psychology Clearinghouse, Eastern Mennonite College, Harrisonburg, Va. 22801.

[3]Available from The Center of Personalized Instruction, Georgetown University, Washington, D.C. 20007.

[4]These are:(a) *The Personalized System of Instruction (PSI): The Keller Plan Applied in Engineering Education,* James E. Stice, ed., Bulletin No. 4. Bureau of Engineering Teaching, College of Engineering, The University of Texas at Austin, December, 1971. (b) *Proceedings of the Keller Method Workshop Conference, Rice University.* A. J. Dessler, ed. Space Science Department, Rice University, Houston, Texas. (c) *The Personalized System of Instruction in Higher Education: Readings on PSI-The Keller Plan.* J. S. Sayre and J. J. Knightly, eds. Enid, Oklahoma: Seminary Press. 1972. (d) *Personalized System of Instruction: 41 Germinal Papers.* J. Gilmour Sherman, ed., Menlo Park, Calif.: W. A. Benjamin, 1974.

The student preference for PSI courses approaches ninety percent, and the grades in PSI course are typically higher than those in traditional courses. The distribution of grades changes from the usual normal distribution or bell-shaped curve, with an average in the C range, to a U-shaped function with a large number of A's. These results have been reported again and again in many disciplines and at all levels of education. Less than ten papers report data differing significantly from these characteristic results. Few problems have been reported, but there are some. (A discussion of the problems can be found in footnote 4d.) The trend now is to accept these positive findings, to ask new questions, and to direct experimentation toward an analysis of the system itself. The defining characteristics of PSI (see Chapter Three) leave room for a variety of decisions concerning implementation, as discussed in Chapter Four. The direction of current research promises to provide data upon which to base some of those decisions.

While the data collected by independent teachers will continue to provide a rich source of information, there is one large-scale research effort worth watching. Dr. James E. Stice, Dr. Billy V. Koen, and their colleagues at the University of Texas at Austin, are engaged in a two-year research project through a grant from the Alfred P. Sloan Foundation. In addition to initiating and developing several PSI courses, their proposal lists nine questions which indicate the direction of this substantial research effort. Their proposal reads in part:

1. Do students learn more (or better) under the Keller Plan than under "conventional" teaching methods?

2. A Keller Plan course produces very different grade distributions than those seen in conventional courses, as many students get A's and B's in a PSI course. Are these higher grades justified? (This is a slightly different question than Number 1 above.)

3. Does the "average" student in a PSI course exhibit a significantly different longterm retention of facts and concepts than the "average" student in a lecture course?

4. We have repeatedly found evidence that students in a PSI course gradually learn how to study efficiently and for meaning rather than depending on their previous experience that memorizing "gets them by." We need documentation on this very important point, and we want to know, does this development of improved ability to learn on one's own transfer to other courses?

5. Can the PSI materials developed by a given professor be used in another university with roughly equivalent results? That is, are well-written PSI courses relatively independent of who the actual

teacher is, provided the teacher using them understands how the Keller Plan works?

6. What are the costs of a Keller Plan course in relation to the costs of lecture courses?

7. The majority of people who have taught PSI courses have experienced the "procrastination problem," evidenced by a significant number of students who progress through the course at a rate much slower than the average. What are the various causes of procrastination, and how may a course be designed to minimize the problem?

8. Connected with Question 7 is the problem of dropouts. PSI courses regularly produce a higher dropout rate than other courses (and almost no failing grades). Can this dropout percentage be reduced, and how?

9. What is the effect of class size? The courses to be developed will range in size from 20 students to 120 students, and Keller suggests that 125 might be the upper limit, since as class size increases the bureaucracy increases, and about 12 proctors may be about all one professor can supervise adequately. Most of the courses we have taught have been in the range of 10-50 students. Does the quality of a PSI course degrade as class size increases from 50 to, say, 120?

Another recent project, the Center for Personalized Instruction at Georgetown University, has quite a different purpose. Jointly funded by the Carnegie Corporation of New York and the Fund for the Improvement of Post-Secondary Education, a part of the Department of Health, Education and Welfare, the Center acts as an information clearinghouse for PSI through workshops, conferences and publications.

The Center developed out of an older project, the *PSI Newsletter*.[5] The *Newsletter,* first sent out in June 1971 reports on conferences, materials available, published articles on PSI, and new PSI courses. The *Newsletter* offers the best record of PSI's development during the past half decade.

PSI is not limited to the United States. As reported in Chapter Two the method had its initial tryout in Brazil, developed in response to a request from the University of Brasília. Our Brazilian colleagues have not been inactive since these early days. Under the leadership of Professor Carolina Martuscelli Bori, PSI has had an independent but

---

[5] The *PSI Newsletter* is available from The Center for Personalized Instruction, Georgetown University, Washington, D.C. 20007

largely parallel development in Latin America. PSI is probably more widely used and better established as a part of the educational system in Brazil than it is in the United States (see Chapter Seven). The achievements of the Brazilians were recognized in February 1973 when UNESCO sponsored a two-week workshop in Brasilia attended by teachers from eleven Latin American countries. This has now been followed by a similar workshop in Venezuela. The Monterrey Institute of Technology in Mexico may have the largest number of concurrently offered PSI courses in any university in the world.

The Monterrey experience suggests one final development, a very recent trend which is actually a return to the original design and intent of PSI. At the outset, PSI was a plan to base educational advancement on accomplishment, rather than on the clock and the calendar. Self-pacing was intended to be exactly that, hardly hampered by boundaries called "courses" and certainly not prohibited by time constraints called "semesters." Few, if any, PSI courses have followed that concept. Most should be called "self-paced *up to a point,*" that point being determined by the registrar, the dean, or whomever we credit with setting the university calendar. The result of this compromise has been that the *Incomplete* policy has become a major issue, and "procrastination" has become the number one problem of discussion in the PSI literature. Recently a few already established colleges have set up a series of PSI courses where students can move ahead as their achievement dictates. Two or three new colleges have been specifically designed on a modular basis where college education will not be a four-year "tour of duty," but will occupy whatever time it may take the student to master the required material. There are other existing proposals for self-paced educational programs administered outside the structure of the traditional educational institutions.

It is these attempts to return to the ideal of truly self-paced education that we should look to as the indicators of PSI tomorrow.

CHAPTER SEVEN

Developments in Brazil

Carolina Martuscelli Bori

In Chapter Six Professor Sherman has noted that PSI in the United States and in Brazil developed in an "independent but largely parallel" manner. To this it might be added that in certain respects the two movements have become more diversified. In this chapter I shall attempt to describe the way that PSI developed in Brazil and to show how this diversity evolved and with what implications.

In August 1963, at the Philadelphia meeting of the American Psychological Association, Professor Keller presented the blueprint of a "more or less imaginary first course in psychology" not yet taught but which was related to the organization of a new psychology department at the University of Brasília (see Chapter Two).[1] This blueprint influenced, and was influenced by, the planning then in progress of an introductory course for that department in which Rodolpho Azzi, Professor Sherman, and I were participating.

---

[1] F. S. Keller. "A Personal Course in Psychology." Paper read on August 31, 1963 at the Philadelphia meetings of the American Psychological Association. Also in *Personalized System of Instruction: 41 Germinal Papers*, J. G. Sherman, ed., Menlo Park, Calif.: W. A. Benjamin, 1974.

The plan that we were formulating, but which was never put into action, included readings, written exercises, laboratory experiments and reports, data analyses, class demonstrations, and a few lectures. After reading the first assignment, the individual student was to be tested on it. If successful, he could attend a lecture or move on to another unit of the course—say an experimental exercise. And so on, at his own pace, until the course work was completed.

This course, as we designed it, had all of the distinctive features which, later on, Professor Keller would formally present in his paper, "Good-bye, Teacher . . ."[2]—small units of reading matter and short laboratory exercises, communication through the written and printed word, lectures and demonstrations as motivational vehicles, and a relative lack of time requirements or deadlines. There were even tutors in this imaginary course during the laboratory hours.

Another aspect of the course deserves particular mention. The planned sequence of topics to be covered by our twenty units was not to be found in any available textbook. The logical sequence of experimentation, reading, and the like which we envisioned could not be carried out. We were therefore compelled to get material from a variety of sources and then divide this into units. In this process, our original sequence was altered and a new one was dictated, not so much by our real objectives as by the available texts. Such a state of affairs is not uncommon with users of PSI today.

The first personalized course actually taught at Brasília in 1964 was an *Introduction to the Analysis of Behavior* (or IAEC-1) and has been briefly described in Chapter Two. The course contained a fair amount of readings, laboratory exercises, some lectures, and a few demonstrations. The program followed the structure of Keller and Schoenfeld's and Holland and Skinner's textbooks which, by then, had been translated into Portuguese. With each assignment the student received a sheet of paper containing a brief account of the task ahead and its relation to the past one. The laboratory instructions followed the model used by Keller and Fields at Columbia College in the fall of 1963 (see Chapter Two). Such detailed instructions were provided because of the limited experience of Brazilian students with this form of independent work and laboratory study. Data treatment and analysis were equally the subjects of specific instructions, and were kept consistent with the goals of the course that we had originally planned.

One aspect of the Brasília course will suggest the value that we placed upon the laboratory experience: whereas quizzes on the reading were graded by a clerk (with the help of a template!), a graduate stu-

---

[2]F. S. Keller. "Good-bye, Teacher . . ." In *Personalized System of Instruction: 41 Germinal Papers.*, J. G. Sherman, ed., Menlo Park: W. A. Benjamin, 1974, Paper No. 1.

dent, specially prepared, monitored the laboratory work of every student. His main function was not related to equipment or procedure, but to data collection and discussions.

Because of the interest aroused in our IAEC-1 and IAEC-2 (which emphasized *human* behavior), the Human Sciences Institute requested a similar course for their students—a shortened version of IAEC-1 and -2. Here the difficulty in selecting texts showed up again. Sequencing raised an even greater problem, since with a shortened course, several steps had to be eliminated.

With the interruption of all academic functions at the University of Brasília in the fall of 1965, personalized instruction in Brazil came to a halt. When it was resumed, a little later, at the Catholic University in São Paulo, it was under very different circumstances and some new ideas. The Psychology Department at that university had not received the laboratory equipment it had purchased, and the experimental emphasis of IAEC could not be implemented. Data had to be separated from procedure in our teaching.

Under such conditions we turned to the experience of Professors Keller (1965) and Sherman (1967) at Arizona State University.[3] We decided to teach the conceptual framework of our course separately from the laboratory practice. This decision affected both the content and the programming of our course. Although students and assistants liked the format, its results were not as satisfactory to us as they had been when the activities of reading and doing were more closely intertwined.

In this same course, another new feature was added. All tests were evaluated, not by a clerk, but by members of the teaching staff. In this process, every answer on a test was discussed with the student in a manner like that described by Keller in 1965 in connection with his treatment of the proctor's function.

These were the first of many changes this course underwent through its use at different colleges and with different students. Some of these adaptations, planned and taught by former tutors at Brasília, kept the principal characteristics of PSI: small-sized units, written communication, alternate test forms, and self-pacing. In the majority of cases, however, the course was borrowed and used because it represented a set of readings selected and adapted for our schools. In fact, most professors were more interested in the content of our course than in our method. Gradually the initials, IAEC-1, took on a meaning more related to a reading list than to the teaching system it originally represented.

---

[3]F. S. Keller. "New Reinforcement Contingencies in the Classroom." Paper read at the New York meetings of the American Psychological Association, August 1965, and J. G. Sherman. "Application of Reinforcement Principles to a College Course." Paper read at American Educational Research Association, New York, February 1967.

By this time, our course was very popular in Brazil. Very few psychology courses were as widely used by so many professors at different schools in our country. Its main effect was to introduce laboratory exercises into the routine teaching of psychology (and, of course, the related spread of operant thinking—reinforcement theory). However, it had little influence on the attitudes of these professors with respect to the teaching of courses other than introductory psychology. Very few of those who used IAEC-1 applied a similar format to new and different courses.

As exceptions to what has just been said there were a few psychology courses in the areas of learning, motivation, and social psychology, at both the graduate and undergraduate levels, whose programming, generally speaking, followed the format of PSI. In addition, there appeared within these courses two new features. First, instead of a paragraph or two of introduction to each reading unit, longer, more detailed instructions were commonly supplied. Objectives for the specific unit were stated, suggestions were offered as to use of the material, and information was furnished concerning the nature and criteria of evaluation. As can be seen, these one-page introductions became quite similar, in scope and detail, to laboratory instructions and, in a sense, they were truly study guides.

The second innovation came with the appearance of the interview technique.[4] When verbal (oral) fluency was thought to be important, the model proposed by Charles B. Ferster was often followed, as a condition of learning and' as a means of its evaluation. This produced some interesting results, since Ferster's structure permitted the shaping of oral fluency while maintaining the characteristics of PSI. The strategy of alternate tests and interviews offers an added virtue: a break with the repetitiveness of continual reading and testing.

------

[4]Editor's note: The interview technique was first used in a PSI course by Dr. C. B. Ferster in an introductory psychology course at Georgetown University in 1967. At the end of each unit, the student finds another student to listen to him describe the concepts he just read. After a limited amount of time, the listener responds to the speaker, commenting on inaccuracies and oversights. The interview is an intermediary step which comes after the student has read the study guide and text and before he has taken the unit quiz. For a more detailed description of the interview technique, consult "Individualized Instruction in a Large Introductory Psychology College Course," by C. B. Ferster, *Psychological Record,* 18, 1968. Reprinted in *Personalized System of Instruction: 41 Germinal Papers,* J. G. Sherman, ed., Menlo Park, Calif.: W. A. Benjamin, 1974, Paper No. 34.

PSI did not immediately find its way into other disciplines. Very few science teachers adopted the system, even though they might have heard about it or seen it in use within psychology departments. Yet there was a climate of dissatisfaction with the state of science teaching in Brazil which showed itself in various ways, ranging from informal meetings and discussions to symposia dealing with the urgent need for methodological innovation. It was in such a context that the Physics Department at the University of São Paulo asked for a course in basic principles of behavior. Such a course was provided, using the Ferster model, and has since been repeated on a number of occasions for students in physics and engineering.[5]

One young man who took this course was Professor I. Iida, of the Polytechnical School at the University of São Paulo. In 1970 he decided to program a course in Human Engineering, based upon the Ferster pattern. Accordingly, the first few interviews on course units were conducted by the professors in charge and, from then on, also by those students who had passed a given unit.

The implications of this course were seen to be great, and the enthusiasm it aroused among the students was even greater. However, the use of students as interviewers led to difficulties as the semester neared its end. With a deadline clearly in sight, the pressure mounted to obtain an interviewer's "pass," and the quality or "noise" in the interviews reached an unacceptable level. In the following semester, this problem was avoided through the use of proctors to carry out the interviews, rather than student interviewers, and in addition, for some units, a written test replaced the interview. Since then, Professor Iida has been responsible for the orientation of several engineering courses, both graduate and undergraduate, at the Federal University of Rio de Janeiro, and now all of the courses employ this same procedure. Professor Iida's work should be of special value, since it represents an inter-departmental effort towards a greater integration of several courses within a technological area.[6]

At about this time in 1972 at the University of Brasília, an introductory course in physics and mechanics was being tried out, using PSI.

---

[5] This course was taught by M. I. Rocha e Silva, who had taught a similar course with Ferster at the University of Maryland and was collaborating with the Department of Experimental Psychology at the University of São Paulo.

[6] I. Iida and M. C. Santoro. "Relatório sobre Aplicação do Método de Ensino Individualizado."Escola Politécnica da Universidade de São Paulo, Junho, 1970 (Paper).

Professor L. C. Gomes, of the Physics Department, had become enthusiastic about the system after reading Keller's "Good-bye, Teacher . . ." Shortly thereafter, at the same institution, PSI was adopted for all the introductory courses in chemistry and mathematics. Before long the system had been applied to a population of four thousand students.

The use of PSI in these courses was limited, however, to the theoretical aspects of the disciplines; all the practical activities, such as the solving of mathematics problems and the carrying out of laboratory exercises, continued to be taught in the classical manner. Also, as might be expected, there were trouble-making features of the applications, most of which were related to the selection and training of proctors. It has been our experience that a familiarity with articles on PSI, although an important determinant in deciding upon its use, is not a sufficient condition for solution of problems of administration and programming of a course.

Nonetheless, the physicists continued to use personalized instruction, adding a new feature. At the Federal University of Rio Grande do Sul and at the University of São Paulo, prior to the introduction of PSI on a large scale, the program was used with a smaller class of students. From this group proctors were chosen and carefully trained. In this way, many problems of implementation could be resolved, at least in part.

In other areas of study, such as social science, several attempts have been made to use PSI, although very few have been personalized all the way. Courses in sociology, anthropology, geography, history, philosophy, and foreign language have employed certain features of the system—small study units and frequent testing, for example—but they have rarely used the plan *in toto*.

Unfortunately, too, in no area of study (psychology, physics, or other) has permission been granted by administrative officials for students to complete their courses outside the rigid limits of the academic semester. Nor has there been an adoption of the alternative solution— the adjustment of course materials or sequence of activities within the established course duration. Consequently, these courses give the impression of being somewhat more teacher-paced than student-paced, and frequently this has brought about changes in mastery criteria and/ or repeated testing possibilities.

Gradually the main difficulties related to the use of PSI in Brazil have shifted from those of course content to those of personnel training. There are enough textbooks and other reading matter to select from. Instructors have developed reasonable proficiency in preparing and presenting such materials—but the fine points of programming and actual course administration continue to suffer from inadequate knowledge and experience. These concerns attested to the need not only for skill in preparing materials and solving practical problems, but for an understanding of the principles underlying PSI.

Two workshops, given during 1972 and 1973 at the Federal University of Goiás and at the Federal University of Bahia, included among its participants a majority of social-science and education professors. These workshops involved, in addition to readings on the major features of PSI and on the making of decisions as to the terminal behaviors sought for, a series of readings on the principles and procedures essential to the effective understanding of programming techniques and PSI logistics. Each member of the workshop group was required to program a course and write its first few units. Since the workshop itself employed the format of PSI, the participants had an opportunity to experience its contingencies and occasionally to serve as proctors. Although this does not completely provide the actual experience of giving a PSI course, it is a good approximation.

Another kind of training has also been tried. This relates specifically to teaching a small group of people, in a short period of time, to plan and write remedial courses on technical subjects.[7] The great success of such training appears to be attributable to the fact that all participants completed their training by actually serving as proctors in the later operation of their courses. We have not yet analyzed the implications of this procedure, but it currently seems to us that the opportunity to prepare a course is not in itself sufficient to assure its later success. It is worth noting, however, that even when the workshop organizer does not check up on the course that is later taught, the results are highly satisfactory: the participants are completely able to plan a course and prepare its material, obeying all the major rules of the PSI format.

Parallel-wise, it has become increasingly clear to us, from analyses and discussions in our "Seminars on PSI" at the University of São Paulo, that "although an elaborate and complicated affair, a system of teaching is presumably reducible to a set of three-term contingencies."[8] It seems to us that if the development of PSI as a system of teaching initially emphasized the format, later on it should increasingly depend upon the potentialities and degree of specification inherent within the learning principles it is derived from.

---

[7]This investigation was sponsored by CENAFOR, a federal government center for the furtherance of professional training.

[8]This is taken from F. S. Keller's *Discussant's Comments* at a symposium on Personalized Instruction, in the August 1971 meeting of the American Psychological Association in Washington, D.C.

Some research in Brazil is currently moving in this direction. The starting point has been a detailed analysis of the activities essential within the program of a course. Such analysis involves a thorough examination of the antecedents of which the specific behavior is a function, the behavior itself, and its consequences. Since the three-term contingency is now our unit of study, the activities themselves no longer maintain their identity. Our work increasingly becomes a study of contingencies.

Plainly speaking, we no longer teach people to program courses, but to search for contingencies within activities, and program *them*. The more elaborate the programming, the more detailed the analysis of the contingencies most frequently found, for example, in laboratory experiments, in graphing, interviewing, reading, writing, and so on. The work already done suggests that the choice of the activities within a course should not be a matter of secondary importance. It could well be one of the principal reasons for the course's success or failure. In other words, the programmer should put into his courses those activities which provide the students with the most opportunities to emit the behaviors of interest. It can be noted, as an example, that *reading* activity, under such analysis, becomes less of a vehicle for content and information and more of an instrument for acquiring behavior.

Disciplines which are programmed with terminal behaviors clearly defined and which employ the results of an analysis such as that outlined above would seem to be an interesting development of PSI. At least they represent a more ambitious stage or programming tactics. The PSI format is followed in such courses, but what is changed within its logistics are the determiners of sequencing.

This concern, reflected in our analyses by the choice of activities within a program, has determined new paths for research on PSI in Brazil. The positive findings in terms of achievement, preference, and students' attitudes towards PSI in more than one country are sufficient to establish the format as an important contribution—worth knowing, keeping, and using. But the implementation of the system calls for more research on the procedures to be used in the evaluation of student performance as determined by the programming contingencies. This evaluation should not be made in terms of subject-matter mastery, but should be based upon the analysis of stimulus conditions and behavioral consequences, with respect to the behavior of the students, the proctors, and the professors themselves.

CHAPTER EIGHT

PSI is not for Everyone

Fred S. Keller

The statements are commonly made and seldom documented that PSI cannot be used in certain courses, by certain teachers, or under this or that condition. To what extent are these assertions true? When is the system not to be prescribed?

The limits of PSI are yet to be established, either with respect to subject matter or level of instruction. The course that is commonly cited as beyond the reach of PSI—in philosophy, language, history, music, or art, for example—often turns out to have been successfully taught by someone. Present indications suggest a far wider range of usage than was originally expected. It is quite clear, however, that for certain teachers and in special situations the procedure ought not to be applied.

The plan should not be used in any course of study wherein subject matter mastery is less important than regular exposure of the student to some charismatic figure, either via formal lectures or in seminar encounters. Professor Crackshaw's disquisitions on the Holy Roman Empire or the analysis of Shakespeare's sonnets by Professor Triller may be so exceptional, may contain so many built-in reinforcements for the listener, as to draw a crowd three times a week or promote a high degree of creative emulation. The virtues of such courses can hardly be compared with those in which there is only an occasional exposure to a lecture or a discussion, as in a course which uses PSI.

The plan was not devised for any teacher who does not wish to let his colleagues know the detailed content of the course he offers—who is unwilling to expose his assignments, his study questions, or his tests to the scrutiny of others. The privacy of the student is protected by the PSI procedure, but that of the teacher is not. Everything he feels to be important is there for all to see, and if a critic indicates an error or an omission, the teacher cannot say, "This was covered in my lectures."

The method will not serve the teacher who believes the student should control the content of the course in which he is enrolled, or the degree to which it shall be understood. Once a student has decided what it is he wants to learn and from whom he wants to learn it, his only option under PSI is to leave the field of study if it fails to hold his interest. The teacher who treats the student best is the teacher who knows exactly what he wants the student to achieve and will accept no less than full achievement. Happily for many courses, one or two well-mastered units may produce a fondness for the subject matter and a willingness to follow the instructor's lead without objection.

At the same time, the method will not suit the teacher who cannot bear honest criticism of his course's detailed content, as provided by his better pupils. Such a teacher would be unable to accept the kind of feedback that is basic to successful operation of the plan. The PSI instructor must be alert to any and every sign of faulty tests, defective study questions, or incomprehensible material to be learned.

PSI is not suggested as a solution to the problem of excessive student number with which many educational institutions are concerned today. Initially it might appear to one who hears about the plan that a single teacher could instruct a thousand students as readily as a hundred, if he had enough assistants, space, facilities, and proctors. The problem here is one of proctors, not of students, and is one of educational control. To how many proctors can the instructor give the kind of guidance and attention needed to assure their optimal performance day by day? In other words, when does the weekly proctors' meeting get unwieldy, permitting questions to go unanswered, errors to go undetected, reports on students to go unheard, and the general exchange of practical experience and useful information to be lost?

Currently the answer to such questions is not entirely clear. In practice, however, it appears that more than ten or twelve proctors are difficult to manage efficiently and intimately in the weekly sessions—an estimate that may derive support from experience with the size of effective small-group seminars. If large numbers *must* be taught and new teachers cannot be employed, the instuctor may resolve the issue by assigning a graduate assistant and a squad of proctors to each hundred of his students, while he looks after the content of the course and oversees its operation. Each assistant, in effect, would then be an instructor, with some autonomy of function, but without the burden of selecting textbooks, preparing units, or constructing readiness tests.

No teacher should attempt to use the plan without the full support of the head of his department, his dean, and other key officials. The PSI instructor must be protected from the criticism of his colleagues and the complaints of functionaries in his institution. When Astronomy 100 is suddenly doubled in enrollment; when the percentage of A's in the course is multiplied by five or more; and when *Incompletes* appear in unprecedented number, one can look for critical comment or the demand for an explanation. At such times the teacher needs protection from someone well informed and highly placed within the system. No amount of enthusiasm, especially from students, and no eloquence in his own defense can equal the persuasiveness of an understanding officer of administration.

No teacher should adopt the plan in order to free himself from teaching, expecting his assistant and his proctors to relieve him from his class commitments and give him time for other things. A good assistant may, and should, take over various functions as a part of his professional training, and even proctors have been known to hold a course together briefly in emergency conditions. But the role of the teacher is not lessened under PSI; it has only been given a different form. As is the case with any other effective system, smooth and efficient operation requires the close attention to his duties from everyone involved, and a deficiency in any function will soon be felt in all the others.

PSI should not be recommended for the use of any teacher who believes that, because of genetic or environmental factors, only a handful of his pupils can ever be deserving of an A or its equivalent. The fact is that we do not know the potential of our student at almost any academic level. The grade-point average, for example, may not tell us how he will progress within a course that uses PSI; and the part played in any classroom by hereditary factors will not be estimated with precision until every student has had a history of learning under optimal conditions. Meanwhile, however, many teachers will not wish to grade their pupils solely on the basis of unit-test performance, with or without a final examination. Such teachers should not be encouraged to adopt the system.[1]

---

[1] Even some of those who claim to use the plan will sometimes add an extra hurdle (for example, a book review, a special project, or a paper) in order to single out their "better" students!

Neither should the plan be tried by any teacher who does not intend to use it as a whole. "Modified" or "partial" PSI is very common, with results that are often better than those obtained before. A cautious teacher, for example, may unitize his course, develop sets of study questions, test his students once a week, provide a make-up quiz for those who fail, and use his lectures for remedial purposes only. The very success of such procedures may block the way to further progress; and any failures that result may be attributed unfairly to the weakness of the plan itself. Better by far that the method first be used *in toto*, if only to test our claims. Once a baseline is established, the effect of a modified procedure can readily be explored.

Finally, PSI is not for the teacher who feels that he is currently successful, that the age-old practices are basically sound or that any faults they have could be repaired with just a little effort. PSI is not for the teacher who is certain that all his problems would disappear if his students were more carefully selected, better trained before they reached him, or had sufficient pressure placed upon them to do the work they should. It is not for any teacher who believes that because he *is* a teacher the system that produced him must be mainly good; that teaching is a game that he must win in competition with his pupils; that lecturing is basic to every teacher's function; that an examination or a quiz is a way of weeding out the weaklings; that any large, strong, well-coordinated boy is probably a moron; that his course may be a measure of I.Q., and that anyone who fails it is unlikely to succeed in later life.

CHAPTER NINE

Afterthoughts and Leftovers

Fred S. Keller and
J. Gilmour Sherman

Behold, the Teacher!

What college teacher do you know who may be called successful with more than a handful of his pupils—not just in leading them to follow his profession, but in teaching them the barest fundamentals of his science or his art, or in simply winning for it their respect?

Regardless of the efforts of the union and the guild, the teacher is still a person of very doubtful status. He is laughed at, mimicked, and lampooned by many; he is lauded, loved, and highly regarded by a few; he is hated heartily by some and is a matter of supreme indifference to countless others. According to reports, he is an absent-minded fumbler, a tyrant, a clown, a weakling, a saint, a wit, a showman, a genius, a charlatan, a dullard, and a guiding light. It is difficult to escape the feeling that only the generosity of the young, the forgetfulness or sentimentality of parents, and the subsidies of government permit him to survive.

FSK

Once More, With Feeling!

The PSI explosion, in this country and in others, has been a source of satisfaction to all of those who played a part in the development of the system. But is is also becoming a source of worry. The designation, PSI, is becoming too inclusive.

The plan that came into being at Arizona State University in 1965-1968, the basic subject matter of this book, has been successfully employed by many teachers since; but the number of those who are using SLI ("something like it"), with less than optimal results, is even greater. Also, and equally disturbing, is the tendency for PSI to be equated with a variety of teaching methods, some of which have little in common with it, either in origin, purpose, or basic format. Regardless of the well-established virtues possessed by such approaches, PSI is not to be identified with token economies, programmed textbooks, learning for mastery, the open classroom, or the audio-tutorial system. These are healthy, sturdy cousins, well able to survive and possibly outlive PSI, but to lump them all together can only lead to trouble.

In 1972 at Rice University, I proposed a recipe to those who would use our plan in courses of their own. It may not be pointless to repeat it here and add some relevant comment. In this way the essentials of PSI may once more be stressed.

"Break down your course material into study units—twenty to thirty in a three-hour course, including three or four units of review." There should be, as Ben Green advises, at least as many units as there are weeks in such a course; anything less is currently undesirable.[1] Billy Koen has some interesting things to say about unit size in this connection.[2] Every move that is made to reduce the number of units in a standard course of any sort is likely to be a move in the wrong direction.

"Add to each unit a set of study questions . . . and make up three or four tests to cover the same material." The study questions should deal with all the important elements of the assignment. In some courses sample problems with their solutions will be included. Test questions,

---

[1]Ben A. Green, Jr., "Suggestions for avoiding problems with PSI—Some do's and don'ts." (An unpublished paper which can be obtained from The Center for Personalized Instruction, 29 Loyola Hall, Georgetown University, Washington, D. C. 20007.)

[2]Billy V. Koen, "Determining unit structure in a PSI course." (Paper delivered at the annual meeting of the American Society for Engineering Education, June 19-22, 1972. Copies may be obtained from Prof. Koen, Department of Mechanical Engineering, University of Texas, at Austin, Austin, Texas 78712.)

or problems, should do the same—sample all important parts of the assignment. If you think you can't do this without an over lengthy test, something is wrong—for example, your units may be too large.

"Put each student through your units at his own pace, testing him as many times as needed, without penalty for failure, until each one is mastered to perfection." Teacher-pacing is a sign of *your* weakness, not the student's, but be sure you give him opportunities enough for testing. *Perfection*, like *mastery*, is a tricky term; if you don't want to get into metaphysics, let it mean what you would call an *A*-performance on your test.

"Throw in a few lectures or demonstrations during the term, for seasoning, but don't require your students to attend them; their aim is to inspire [or to enrich], not to be remedial or to inform" This reduction in your talking time will make you feel guilty for awhile and may draw a few complaints from the nestlings in your class, but you and they will soon recover.

"Use well-prepared and carefully guided student proctors to grade the unit tests. One proctor to each ten students is about the right proportion." Moreover, you can handle no more than ten or fifteen proctors in your weekly briefings, if you expect to keep your course in hand. Don't let your proctors "help" their charges overmuch. For any student seeking aid on complicated problems, someone more experienced than the proctor should be on hand to give it—for example, you.

"Add a final examination if you wish, when the units have been completed; it may make your course smell better to your colleagues, or it may fortify the product." As a rule of thumb, don't let this examination carry more than twenty-five or thirty percent of the student's final grade. Give more and you reduce the importance of passing the units; give less and you will put too much burden on the proctors. If the final examination is foregone, its teaching function can be carried out by well-planned units of review.'

"Give an *A* to everyone who completes the course, early or late, as you would a Ph.D. Be generous with your *Incompletes* . . ." The earlier advice at this point was to "stir up things a bit if you see procrastination." This advice should probably be withdrawn. If you have done everything else correctly, you won't have many *Incompletes*. (See the item in this chapter on *Procrastination*.)

"Watch carefully while cooking." PSI is no excuse for abdicating your responsibilities as a teacher just because you do not lecture as you did before; it simply gives you a different task to carry out, as a manager or engineer of learning. If you are concerned with the education of your pupils, you have a chance to show it in new and more fulfilling ways.

FSK

What's New About PSI?

Except in its relation to reinforcement theory, there may be nothing really new in PSI. The system seems to have been developed in practically its present form by Mary Ward in 1912, as described in Chapter Two, and even in more recent days it has been independently hit upon by others. The method used by Helen Mills and her collaborators at American River College, California, in teaching English composition has all the fundamental features of our system, including that of student proctors.[3] It would be folly to assert that other teachers, in other places, have not made similar discoveries.

In most of these developments, however, an important element is missing. A case in point is that of the *correspondence school* technique. If this form of instruction, one finds "(1) specially prepared materials, written in a self-explanatory fashion and arranged into a series of lessons; (2) supplementary printed and other materials; (3) a series of exercises to be worked out by each student; (4) the evaluation of these exercises by a competent instructor with the student being informed of this evaluation and, occasionally, being given the opportunity to correct his errors; and (5) a final examination over the whole course." In addition, "the student may start at any time, study anywhere he wishes and proceed at his own rate of progress."[4] Except for unavoidable lapses of time (between testing and grading, for example) and the *absence of student proctors,* the system sounds a lot like PSI.

Within the universities and secondary schools, imaginative teachers have from time to time uncovered most of the practical rules of PSI and have effectively applied them. The work of Olgierd Celinski, at the University of Ottawa, in Canada, is an especially good example.[5] As early as 1963 Celinski taught a self-paced course in electrical engineering which seems to have met all the requirements of PSI save one—the use of proctors, which he nevertheless suggested as useful in large classes. Celinski's work was never given the attention it deserved, possibly because the time for teaching innovation was not yet ripe.

Less obvious near-discoveries of the plan turn up frequently enough to keep us modest. One claimant of attention, developed at the highschool level and from a project orientation (the construction of an

---

[3] A good account of this procedure is contained in H. Mills, *Commanding Communication—Individualized Instruction in Sentence Writing (Teacher's Manual)*, Carmichael, Calif.: Quest Publishers, 1972.

[4] Cyril O. Houle, In the *Encyclopaedia Brittanica,* 14th ed., s.v. "Correspondence Instruction."

[5] O. Celinski, "Announced Repetitive Tests," In *Personalized System of Instruction: 41 Germinal Papers,* J. G. Sherman, ed. Menlo Park, Calif.: W. A. Benjamin, 1974, Paper No. 31.

electric motor) in industrial arts, is that proposed by Byron M. Taylor in the early thirties.[6] In Taylor's "Integrative Procedure," which had its roots in R. H. Wheeler's "organismic psychology" (a version of Gestalt), one can find most of the features of PSI, together with a number of Gestalt conceptions.

In almost all the cases that have come to our attention (including the one just mentioned), the missing feature seems to be the student proctor, a not-to-be-underestimated aspect of our system. The proctor is the mediating figure, the bridge that helps to span the pupil-teacher gap of understanding, and the one who gives a vital and "contemporary" meaning to the educational process. This difference between PSI and other systems of instruction disappears only when our student is so far advanced (or our teacher is so unpracticed) that face-to-face interaction of the two is intellectually valuable for each. Then the proctor isn't needed.

FSK

"It's a Lot of Work!"

Users of PSI are wont to mention the work that it entails, "especially on the first time around." The Puritan in them is thus appeased, they are vested in nobility of a sort, and drudgery is suggested—continuous, dreary, and dispiriting. The listener-lecturer is led to return to his chores, the administrator to admire this hardy innovator.

There is no question about the time involved in teaching via PSI. Hours should be released for introducing such a course on the first time around and even later, although we lack the data for an exact prescription.[7] There is more than this, however, to the story, and something of a fraud may be involved! The user of the system may have been having more fun than he ever had before in teaching, in spite of the time that he expends. His proctors have become a source of satisfaction as he notes their increased understanding and enjoyment of their function; he knows the strength and weakness of his course material as he never has before; and he may relish his increased acquaintance with his pupils. He

---

[6] B. M. Taylor, "Integration in the Classroom" *California Journal of Secondary Education,* 1935, April, 283-286. "An Integrative Procedure for Industrial Arts," *California Journal of Secondary Education,* May 1937, 290-292.

[7] Charles H. Roth (University of Texas at Austin) found that he averaged thirty-two hours a week on his first PSI course in electrical engineering, which suggests a major effort.

may even find some pleasure in other aspects of his teaching—such as constructing questions like the following:

> Ole Oleson, highballing Norwegian engineer, is driving a fast freight north along a track at a speed of 30 m/sec. Michael O'Flaherty, highballing drunkard, is driving a passenger express at 40 m/sec south along the same track. When the trains are 1.0 km apart, both engineers apply their brakes: Ole decelerates at 3 m/sec^2, Michael at 2 m/sec^2. (a) Do the trains collide or not? (b) Can you adapt a famous line from Kipling to summarize your answer? [8]

FSK

Early Extensions of PSI

The earliest use of PSI with highschool students was probably by J. L. Michael[9], at Grinnell College, Iowa, in 1965. Professor Michael, then at Arizona State University, taught a two-week course in the principles of behavior to selected highschool juniors enrolled in a Behavior Science Institute sponsored by the National Science Foundation and directed by Dr. Neil D. Kent.

Michael's course had ten units, patterned on those developed by Sherman and Keller at Arizona State. Two college students and five members of the class itself were used as proctors (those who were the first to pass through Unit 1). Lectures were provided for those students who were thought to be progressing at a reasonable speed. The results of the experiment were highly gratifying. Michael writes (in a personal communication):

> The students worked very hard on the units and seemed to reach a somewhat higher level of accomplishment than I remember having produced with the traditional lecture method when I taught Psychology 112 to A.S.U. students over an entire semester. Of course the highschool students

---

[8] John T. Bethell, "Teach Yourself Physics in Your Spare Time." *The Harvard Bulletin* 73, No. 3, November, 1972, pp. 30-35. (This article is a description of PSI courses taught by Paul Bamberg and several other teachers. The answers to the questions were: (a) *No,* and (b) *Norse is norse and souse is souse, and never the twains shall meet.*)

[9] Professor Michael, now at Western Michigan University (as is Dr. Kent), in Kalamazoo, Mich., is highly regarded as a teacher of reinforcement theory. He received the American Psychological Foundation's Distinguished Teaching Award in 1971.

spent about ten hours a day on this material and had little else to occupy them during the two-week period, and in addition, they were highly selected highschool students. Still, everyone associated with the Institute was impressed with the excellent effect one could have with individual study and with "keeping up with the group" as the principal motivational device.

Later in the same summer, Michael used the PSI procedure successfully again, in teaching the analysis of behavior to the staff of the Parsons State Hospital and Training School (Parsons, Kansas), all of whom were college graduates. Also, in the spring of 1966, at Arizona State, he taught a course in advanced statistics with the plan. Two more probable firsts were thus achieved.

FSK

Ten Good Tips for Anyone Who Plans to Try Out PSI [10]

1. Choose good readable texts and references, written at the student's level.

2. Make the first units easy, to build confidence; increase difficulty gradually.

3. Avoid including too much material in each unit; the units have to appear manageable to the students.

4. Include review material in problem assignments and quizzes, when possible.

5. Make quizzes as comprehensive and consistent with unit objectives as possible, yet as brief as possible for most rapid grading.

6. Make use of faster students [not proctors] to tutor slower ones.

7. Encourage feedback from the faster students so that reading materials or quizzes can be revised if necessary to make them more effective for the later students.

8. Keep a separate folder of quizzes and a program chart for each student, and provide an area where students can review the contents of their folders.

---

[10] This excellent list of pointers is taken from a very useful and well-written study by D. K. Lewis and W. A. Wolf (Colgate University, Hamilton, N.Y.) in the *Journal of Chemical Education* (1973, 50, No. 1, 51-56) which could profitably be read by any prospective user of PSI, regardless of his special field of study.

9. Choose tutors carefully (in descending order of importance, they should be dependable, articulate, willing to admit what they don't know, and knowledgeable). Reward them appropriately; they are the keys to success of the system.

10. Start small, and be prepared for a large initial expenditure of time writing assignments and quizzes.

FSK

"What About the Hawthorne Effect?"

When any method of training or teaching is described in which there is improved performance of some practical function when new procedures have been used or new conditions of working have been imposed, you can expect to hear the words "Hawthorne effect." The implication of this utterance is that the positive results obtained may have had little or no relation to the experimental variables supposedly at work. Sometimes it is suggested that the results were due to novelty alone and will not hold up with continuance of the method or conditions.

The term comes from a pioneer investigation at the Hawthorne plant of the Western Electric Company in Chicago, in 1924-32, which dealt with production rates in several skilled activities (relay assembly, mica splitting, bank wiring) under various working conditions (for example, different intensities of illumination). Because of the magnitude of this research and the inaccessibility of complete reports upon it; because of the dramatic nature of some (not all) of its results; and because of the apparent propensity of human beings to find pleasure in the unexpected and mysterious, there has grown up through the years the practice of calling upon the ghost of Hawthorne when we do not care to examine, or would like to discount the claims of, any new departure in the realm of human engineering.

The Hawthorne studies were carried out before the days of reinforcement theory, hence the *consequences* of behavior—the results of "feedback," whether in the form of information on one's progress, an increase in one's pay or status, or some other reinforcer—were unappreciated by researchers as a determinant of output. H. M. Parsons, in a recent paper, has brought the matter up to date and, incidentally, laid the ghost.[11] His principal findings may be summarized as follows.

---

[11] H. M. Parsons, "What Happened at Hawthorne?" *Science*, 183, No. 4127, March 8, 1974.

1. Some of the conditions altered in the Hawthorne studies led to no improvement in performance, or even to a negative effect—not all changes served to raise the output of the workers.

2. Increased productivity did take place, however, which could not be traced specifically to the manipulated variables employed in these researches. This became the "Hawthorne effect."

3. A close inspection of experimental operations in these classic studies reveals a compounding factor, the effect of an additional variable, unrecognized by the researchers, which Parsons calls "a combination of information feedback and financial reward." When this factor is appreciated, the mystery disappears and the variable becomes of research interest in itself.

FSK

Can Everyone Be Educated?

Perhaps not. The nature-nurture, heredity-environment debate has been with us a long time, and is not about to go away. Nor can it be resolved here. However, the belief that some small segment of the population appears to be uneducable should not be used to justify an educational system directed primarily toward selection.

The selection model excuses the teacher from any feeling of responsibility to see to it that his students learn. If the task is to identify "those who have it," it is not difficult to discover that most children do not know very much. If any part of the selection that goes on in our schools is, in fact, related to heredity, the selection procedures used would not satisfy the geneticist. We should only sacrifice our students on the altar of poor genes as a last resort. In the meantime we should teach like hell to prove them innocent of inherited flaws. Selection is not teaching.

In another sense the selection model is just poor experimental design. If there are inherited differences that cannot be overcome, the way to prove it is to assume the opposite, try all alternatives, and fail. The scientist-statistician calls this assuming the null hypothesis, the lawyer terms it the presumption of innocence, the logician speaks of avoiding a self-fulfilling prophecy. It is, as well, a more humane way to treat all our children. We have a lot of alternatives to try before we can in good conscience pre-judge a sizable percentage of our population.

JGS

On Mastery

At times there appears to be some confusion about the meaning of the word *mastery*. Comments such as "some students don't need to know *all* about a subject, they only want to sample it" indicates such a misconception.

Mastery learning does not mean exploring a subject deeply or having all the knowledge possessed by the expert. It does mean the opposite of sloppy, whatever the level. It involves learning well everything that is assigned, without implications that the assignment is elementary or advanced or that the course is a survey or intensive.

Mastery learning of first-grade arithmetic carries no implication that the student who completes the course has learned all of mathematics. He has learned all of the first course and is ready for the second. At this level every student probably needs to learn everything designated as first level math and we probably need only one course for everyone. It may well be that in some subjects at the highschool and college levels two or more alternative courses should be offered—one for the pre-professional student, the other for students only seeking an aquaintance with the topics of the discipline. Mastery learning does not imply choosing one course over the other; rather it suggests a student's work should not be slipshod in either.

Whether directed toward intensive pre-professional training or a general survey for the interested layman, there are advantages to a mastery versus a hit-and-miss approach. It is useful to both student and teacher to know what in fact the student has learned. This is particularly so when there is any possibility of further inquiry into the subject. Students completing traditional courses are more often unique in what they haven't learned than what they have learned. Future study is difficult to prescribe when based on unknown pockets of ignorance.

In the affective domain, mastery learning gives the student a sense of accomplishment which is more likely to lead to sustained interest in the subject matter and an increased desire for further learning than is instruction with a lesser goal. The success involved also has benefits of a more personal kind described by such qualities as confidence and self-esteem.

The call for mastery leads to both proficiency and dignity at any level. Far from being an unreasonable demand it is a disservice to settle for less.

JGS

"That's Fine For Rote Learning—But What About Creativity?"

Oh, to have a dollar for each time some form of that question has been asked! Unfortunately, it is often impossible to detect whether the inquisitor is teasing or sincere.

In one case the question is asked cloaked in the guise of calling for originality. The sophisticated analyst knows he is dragging out a surefire red herring; it is a calculated ploy. Stephen Potter[12] would have listed this as gambit number one for the educational gamesman. Having studied the matter, with a cynical knowledge that no one (including himself) has a final answer, the questioner has several fallback positions. "Can you program another Mozart or another Shakespeare?" is a popular, if not too imaginative, second-or-third-round question. In asking the question, our champion of the finest in scholarship can't lose. In fact, asking it will probably win him the appreciation of those genuinely concerned with higher level cognitive skill. He is playing to that audience.

How do we answer his question? Calling him a fraud appears to impugn the ambitions of the sincere and to advocate transforming education into the rote memorization of facts. His question is a neat trick, perpetrated by a charlatan, and difficult to expose. Yet, the sincere inquirer deserves an answer—an answer that must include a recognition of the highest levels of human achievement. It must acknowledge that we have no proven formula for the training or creation of those rare individuals we distinguish with the label, "genius." It should make equally obvious that traditional education also does not have that formula. Otherwise there would be a lot more geniuses.

This is not to deny an interest in teaching conceptualization, critical thinking, originality, inventiveness, and other good things. It is only to point out that the challenge given to PSI has not been answered by traditional education. This may be revealed by turning the question back to the person who asked it. He may claim to nurture "something more creative" but fumble a lot when asked what it is he is nurturing, or how he is doing it. His teaching goals, when examined, appear to exclude by definition anything that can be defined. The questioner assumes that to get a handle on any new complexity is to reduce it to rote learning. This leaves untouched his quest for the stimulation of unique inquiry.

As long as the goal is "that certain *je ne sais quoi*," defined as that

---

[12] Stephen Potter, *Some Notes on Lifemanship.* London: Rupert Hart-Davis, 1952.

which cannot be specified, the argument is secure, hopeless, and uninteresting. When the critic tells us what it is he wants to teach, in behavioral terms rather than in metaphors, there is a very good chance we can design a PSI course that will lead students to learn the desired behavior. In the meantime, we must leave the critic to his doggedly defended, unreachable aims, noting only that when he describes how he stimulates individual inquiry it sounds very much as if he is recommending a brief sojourn into the world of individualized instruction in behalf of those few students he feels deserve it. He may even complain that his normal teaching duties leave him too little time to engage in this creative type of individualized teaching.

After pointing out that there are those who shout "rote learning" almost by rote, and admitting there are no PSI courses that can produce a generation of Nobel Laureates, it is only fair to indicate that some complex cognitive and affective results have been achieved. There is no limitation on what can be taught other than the provision that we must be able to state the objectives of instruction in terms of the performance desired. Initially, instructors taught what was most easily specified. Science and mathematics led the way but others followed. The social sciences and humanities have accomplished what might have been thought impossible only three or four years ago. English and philosophy teachers claim it is not only possible to use PSI to teach the abstract interpretive skills involved in their fields, but that their disciplines profit from the analysis of information the exercise of specifying objectives demands. It may be that there is no barrier to teaching creativity other than the ingenuity of those designing the courses!

One goal of education, clearly beyond rote learning, deserves special attention. A frequent report from students in PSI courses is that they learn how to study. A few creative teachers have taken this observation seriously and, wishing to develop that skill, have deliberately created course sequences which decrease the instructions and the support provided by them at a rate determined by the progress of the student. Teaching students how to learn independently, and awakening in them a desire to do so, could well prove as important an accomplishment as any "creative" teaching now going on.

The PSI teacher has two other advantages as he attempts to stimulate originality. One is that, having provided a written guide to predictable problems, he is free to devote his time to students with unique problems. Thus while the PSI teacher may be as busy as his more traditional colleague, he need not deal with redundant tasks (his proctors handle that), which limit the time he can devote to those individual students who need, want, and deserve his help. He can now spend most of his time working with such students. While others applaud the creative, and deplore how little attention they can direct toward developing it, the PSI teacher has created a system which allows him more time to do just that.

Finally, by working within a system that leaves a record, is cumulative, and can be replicated, the PSI teacher is in a position to improve his own teaching and to profit from the experiences of others. PSI makes the procedures of learning visible. We can be modest in our claims of achievement and confident in a technique that will show progress. The sincere teacher should know that now there is a systematic way to explore instruction—instruction with increasingly complex goals.

JGS

Large Scale Implementation

Most comments in this book concern single courses. To date we have limited experience with departments that offer several PSI courses or with colleges that have implemented PSI on a broad scale. However, it is clear that new opportunities arise when many PSI courses exist within the same institution.

When several courses within a prerequisite structure are taught by PSI, self-pacing can actually occur. Semesters no longer determine what a student will study and students can proceed from one course to the next on the basis of accomplishment. When such a program extends to an entire curriculum, a college degree need not be synonymous with four years on campus.

Multiple PSI offerings create new options for the student. He may study one course at a time, presumably proceeding rapidly, or enroll in several courses concurrently. Learners can elect a program that matches their personal preferences for concentration or diversification of effort.

As the number of PSI courses increases, new content combinations become possible. Individual units or sequences of units from different courses may fit together to constitute novel areas of study. The possibilities for new inter-disciplinary concentrations, a fresh look at course content, even an analysis of knowledge are but potentials at this point. I suspect these and other as yet unforseen benefits of large scale implementation may be among the more exciting developments of PSI's second decade.

JGS

Procrastination

With true self-pacing there can be no deadline; without a deadline there can be no procrastination. When a student is told, "You must complete your course by the end of the term," or at some later date, a deadline is asserted and the way is paved to procrastination.

Self-pacing is at odds with prevailing educational practice. The postponement of study under our plan may disrupt the school's bookkeeping and recording systems. It gives the computer indigestion, so to speak, and this malaise can be readily transmitted to headquarters. We cannot live successfully by the calendar if too many *Incompletes* are on our rolls.

Since most of us are understandably cowards in this situation, we accept some cut-off date or introduce some other time restrictions. In some degree we compromise, and then discover that we have procrastination. After that, we do what we can to serve two masters. We try to maintain the basic features or our plan while meeting the requirements of the traditional system; and we may to some extent succeed in doing so.

Procrastination, in this quasi-PSI, may be related to one or more of several factors about which something can be done: (1) The units of our course may be too large, especially at its beginning. An assignment that can be mastered in two hours will fit within a student's daily activities better than one that asks for four. It may arouse less fear and less avoidance of the task, and it can more easily compete with other time-consuming and equally rewarding matters. (2) The unit or units may be too difficult in content, producing successive failure and lengthening the time required to pass. (3) The material to be studied may lack intrinsic interest (may have too few built-in reinforcements) and be unable to compete with more absorbing matters in the academic sphere or elsewhere.

These are not the only reasons for delay in taking or passing tests, but they are fairly common ones and should be considered by the teacher before he looks for some inherent weakness in the student and begins to think of "taking steps." The *size* of the unit can usually be reduced, and "easy" units may be used at first, with encouragement to get going. The *difficulty* of the unit can readily be detected and corrected by a teacher who is alert to his pupils' reactions and the reports he gets from his proctors. Supplements can be written for murky sections of a textbook, or alternative materials can be provided.

A common response to "PSI" procrastination is to reduce the possibility of self-pacing even further. Attendance at study hall may be demanded of those who lag behind; course grade may be lowered in proportion to the number of units missing at the end of the term; some kind of "doomsday criterion" may be introduced; and other schemes may be employed.[13]

---

[13]One of the better methods is that employed by C. H. Roth at the University of Texas (Austin). All students are required to come to class for study until Unit 3 is passed. "From then on, the PSI method provides adequate motivation, and attendance is not required." (Roth, C. H. "Continuing Effectiveness of Personalized Self-Paced Instruction in Digital Systems Engineering." *Engineering Education*, 1973, 63, No. 6, 447-450.)

Less aversive methods may include a reduction in the amount of course material in order to get more students under the wire before the term is over; extension of testing-and-grading sessions for some days beyond the term's official end, usually before submitting grades; and reducing the number of *credits* for a course without reducing the grade. These manoeuvres, like the others, are compromises with a system which says that a course of study should always be of fixed duration; that it must start on a given date and be completed on another; and that, except in extreme cases, all students can then be moved ahead to higher-level courses regardless of what their deficiencies may be.

Within this framework of a standard quarter or semester, the self-pacing feature of PSI requires the student's regulation of his own behavior far more than in the traditional teacher-paced system. In a one-term course using PSI, the simple fact of thirty units in a fifteen-week span is enough to cue the student to aim for two units a week. The added nudge provided by a progress chart or a progress curve for the class or for himself may help him to control his study time, to work more at the pace of others, and to maintain, in some degree, the *status quo*. But this cannot be the ideal of a truly self-paced system, and may serve only to delay the student's growth in self-control and self-reliance. At best it is a procedure of transition.

The time is fast approaching for a reevaluation of what constitutes a course of study, when it may be taken and by whom, what credit (if any) should be given for its completion, and how it should be paid for. When these things have taken place, procrastination will be the least important of our problems.

FSK and JGS

"The Proof . . ."

Any success of PSI within the years to come will depend on the number of those who try it out, like it, and pass the word along. It won't be the result of group comparisons of subject-matter mastery, and the "instant analysts" will not have the final say. It will not depend upon statistics or a vote of confidence from some *ad hoc* committee. It won't be due to advertising or the eloquence of its promotors, and it will not take place through *fiat*.

"*The proof of the pudding is in the eating,*" said Sancho Panza. If the system is good, it will survive; if it is bad, it will have to go. We would be pleased to think that we had made it easier for students to learn and teachers to teach; that we had given pride of accomplishment to one and dignity to the other. But if we fail we shall not be the first to do so.

FSK

For more information . . .

The literature on PSI is growing at such a rapid rate that any summary thereof is quickly out of date. For the reader who wishes to investigate the system further, it is suggested that he apply for information to the *Center for Personalized Instruction*, 29 Loyola Hall, Georgetown University, Washington, D.C., 20007. The Center publishes a quarterly *PSI Newsletter* ($3.00 yearly), a set of selected papers, and a regularly updated bibliography of publications dealing with the plan.

INDEX

Page number in bold denotes major discussion of topic.

About the authors . . .

FRED. S. KELLER received his Ph.D. from Harvard University in 1931. He has taught at Colgate, Columbia, the University of São Paulo (where he was a Fulbright Professor), the University of Brasília, Arizona State, and Western Michigan University. Since 1964, he has been a Professor Emeritus at Columbia University. In 1970, he received the Distinguished Teaching Award from the American Psychological Foundation. He is currently on the staff of the Center for Personalized Instruction, Georgetown University, Washington, D.C.

J. GILMOUR SHERMAN earned his Ph.D. in Psychology at Columbia University in 1959. He has taught at Barnard College, the University of São Paulo (as a Fulbright Professor), and helped set up a new Department of Psychology at the University of Brasília. He has since taught at Arizona State and Georgetown University. As a Director of the Center for Personalized Instruction, he edits the quarterly *PSI Newsletter* and participates in PSI conferences and workshops across the country.

3287347